Finding God in a Holy Place

Finding God in a Holy Place

Explorations of Prayer in Durham Cathedral

Chris Cook

mowbray

Published by the Continuum International Publishing Group Ltd
Published by Mowbray, a Continuum imprint
The Tower Building, 11 York Road, London SE1 7NX
80 Maiden Lane, Suite 704, New York NY 10038

www.continuumbooks.com

First published 2010

British Library Cataloguing-in-Publication Data
A catalogue record for this book is available from the British Library.

ISBN 9781906286200

Typeset by Pindar NZ, Auckland, New Zealand
Printed and bound by MPG Books Group Ltd

Contents

This book is dedicated to my mother, who loved holy and beautiful places.

Jesus said to Martha, 'I am the resurrection and the life. Those who believe in me, even though they die, will live, and everyone who lives and believes in me will never die.'

Jn 11.25–26

Foreword

It is an incomparable privilege to be Dean in a Cathedral such as Durham. To live, work and pray in such surroundings is both a daily delight and an awesome responsibility. The danger is that you take for granted a building that is nothing short of a miracle, stop noticing what makes it so extraordinary as architecture and so powerful as a spiritual statement.

This is why Chris Cook's book is a real gift to all who love holy places and love Durham in particular. He invites us on a journey of discovery as a result of which we learn to *see* differently. If it isn't too obvious a cliché, our way of experiencing a building becomes a *pilgrimage*, an exploration. Even the familiar may strike us in new, surprising, even startling, ways. In a great phrase of Wordsworth, we 'see into the life of things' – not only the life of a particular place and the people associated with it, but most of all, our own selves.

Inevitably, Professor Cook's book is written very personally. It is an extended reflection on his own experience of Durham Cathedral. We shall all, no doubt, experience it differently, have our own 'take' on it. That is the richness of being human. But the pages that follow offer us, whoever we are, a method by which to undertake this kind of prayerful, spiritual exercise. This book will be a worthy, and unusual, addition to the literature on sacred places, and on Durham Cathedral in particular. I commend it with enthusiasm and warmth and thank the author for this labour of love.

Michael Sadgrove,
July 2009

Preface

I have written this book because of my experiences of a particular holy place, Durham Cathedral. At first I simply enjoyed arriving a little early for Morning Prayer, to allow some time to sit quietly in preparation. Then I realized that I wanted to spend longer, and that this was somewhere in which my prayers somehow grew more readily, rather like young plants in a greenhouse. Soon, I found that different places within the Cathedral had different things to say about prayer, and that I encountered God in each of them – but differently. Then I realized that somehow the building spoke to me not only about its own past, and about God, but also about me.

The more I thought about all of this, the more I realized that although on the one hand Durham Cathedral is completely unique, on the other hand it was only helping me to explore prayer in ways that didn't require me to be in Durham Cathedral at all, and that it helped me to pray at other times and in other places. This in turn led to a reflection on what it is that makes some places seem especially 'holy'. After all, God is everywhere, so in a very important sense every place is holy.

As far as the Cathedral itself is concerned, I have written about my own reflections, and about how things have appeared to me to be. What I have seen will doubtless be different to what others see. For example, one reader, who knows the story of Margaret of Scotland better than I do felt that my comments about her in Chapter 6 were a bit harsh. Undoubtedly, Margaret had an incredibly difficult life and achieved much in a world dominated by men. But my reflections here are more about a visual image portrayed by an artist than they are about an historical figure and they tell you only about my response to that painting. Doubtless everyone who views it has their own response to it, and these responses tell us much more about ourselves than they do about Margaret of Scotland or even the artist.

Because such a large and old building must have meant so many things to so many different people, what I describe can only be very

partial. My reflections and contemplations might therefore be understood as being merely one very small and broken piece of glass in a
very large and beautiful stained glass window. Doubtless, I will fail to
do justice even to this. It is an attempt to share in words something
that is more or less ineffable and therefore beyond words. However, I
have been fascinated by other people's attempts to describe their ineffable experiences, and have found encouragement in what they have
written. Similarly, I hope that, amidst and despite the inadequacy of
what I write, some things may be said which will be helpful to others.

Like Durham Cathedral, prayer is a beautiful place to explore. This
book does not require that you visit Durham – although I hope that
many readers may. It is rather offered as a kind of introduction to
exploring some different kinds of prayers in different places, and it is
written also with different kinds of people in mind.

So, this book is about prayer, and particularly prayer considered
in the context of place. If prayer is a 'place', it is a place in which we
hope to find God. The book offers meditations upon themes that are
associated with a particular place but is also intended to be a guide to
exploring prayer in the context of places more generally. It could be
used as a resource for a quiet day, or for a retreat or pilgrimage, either in
Durham or elsewhere. I hope that others will find some encouragement
from it as a spur to exploring many different kinds of Christian prayer
in many different places.

Acknowledgements

I am enormously grateful to the Dean and Chapter of Durham Cathedral for their support and encouragement as I have undertaken the task of writing this book. Lilian Groves, the chief guide at Durham Cathedral, has kindly corrected my errors of historical detail. My thanks must go to Jeff Hewitt, the head verger, and his team, for they have often welcomed me early in the morning and have assisted in various small but important ways. My gratitude must be expressed also to members of the Cathedral staff and congregation with whom I have prayed day by day.

Perhaps I would never have written this book at all, but for a conversation with the Dean of Durham, Michael Sadgrove, after he had come to bless our new home in Durham. Ordinary places are made holy by prayer, and it was this that led to the writing of this book.

The photographs used inside the book are my own, and I am very grateful to the Dean and Chapter of Durham Cathedral for their permission to use them here.

I am grateful to Nicola Slee for allowing me to quote her prayer to Mary in Chapter 5, and to Rosalind Brown for allowing me to quote a verse from one of her hymns in Chapter 6. I have tried to contact Josef Pyrz for permission to use his poem (in Chapter 5) but so far without success. I would be pleased to hear from him if he would like to contact me. The hymn and the prayer attributed to St Columba in Chapter 6, appear to be in the public domain, and I have not been able to identify any owners of copyright. I would be pleased to hear from anyone who may know differently.

The plan on p. xii is taken from Baedeker (1910).

I am grateful to Lilian Groves for permission to quote in Chapter 3 her story of the response of a nine-year-old child to the nave.

The translation of the Latin inscription over the Great West Door, given in Chapter 4, was kindly provided by Dr Diana Barclay.

I am grateful to Cuthbert and Bede and all the northern saints, whose examples have been an inspiration and encouragement to me in my Christian pilgrimage. I am grateful to Joy, Andrew, Beth and James, Rachel, and Jonathan, for their company on that pilgrimage as a family.

Many thanks go to Michael Sadgrove, Lilian Groves, Jeff Sandoz, my wife Joy, and two anonymous readers for reading and commenting on different parts of the manuscript. I am especially thankful to Caroline Chartres and her colleagues at Continuum, who gave invaluable advice and encouragement in preparing the manuscript for publication. Of course, any remaining errors and imperfections are mine, but without their help there would have been many more of them!

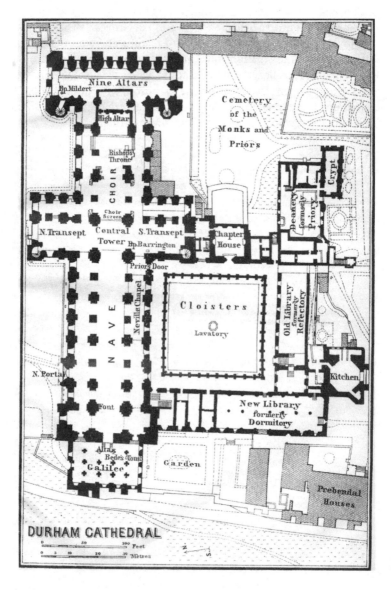

A plan of Durham Cathedral

Chapter 1

Finding a Holy Place: Durham Cathedral

I'll never forget my first ever view of Durham Cathedral – many years ago now –when I was on a train journey to Scotland. As the line turns east into Durham it approaches the north side of the city on a high viaduct. The ground all around drops away and the Cathedral can be seen standing above the city on the rock of the sandstone peninsula. It is a breathtaking view and, having seen it again and again on many train journeys since then, I never cease to be moved by it. On that first encounter, I was drawn by the mysterious beauty of a holy place that I had never seen before. Today the same vista welcomes me home.

It was only many years after that first encounter that I went inside Durham Cathedral for the first time. Just as the outside of the Cathedral is breathtaking, so is the inside. As most visitors are given entry from the west end, the first view is usually of the nave, looking eastwards towards the high altar and the rose window high in the east wall. Within the huge space created by the simple but enormous architecture, the light penetrating from outside through multiple tiers of windows paints a picture of inner holiness which is both humbling and captivating.

Having been inspired by my initial impressions of this cathedral, I went on to deepen the acquaintance. Cuthbert's tomb, the cloisters, the huge central tower with its high belfry and views of Durham, the Chapter House, the monks' dormitory, the great kitchen and other chapels and features of this wonderful building all have their own impressions to create, their own story to tell. Over the years since I first moved to Durham in 2003, I have continued to explore these different facets of the building that sits enthroned upon the rock in the heart of the city, and I continue to be fascinated by them.

Of course, greater familiarity reveals that there are dark corners and less presentable sides to this beautiful place. The Cathedral that towers towards heaven, proclaiming the glory of God, was also once a visible symbol of Norman political power in the north of England. This holy

1

place of worship was used in 1650, following the battle of Dunbar, as a prison for 3,000 Scottish soldiers. But, somehow, this dark side to the Cathedral only enhances the mystery and relevance of its message. The four gospels do not fail to tell us about the human hypocrisy, deceitfulness and cruelty which greeted the truth, grace and self-giving that were made incarnate in the humanity of Jesus of Nazareth. Neither does this building fail to remind us that the very best aspects of human nature are sometimes closer than we care to admit to the very worst parts of ourselves, those parts that we would prefer to deny.

This is also a point at which to pause and acknowledge that the Cathedral has its own mythology, a mythology which includes a collection of stories and fables that do not always match with reality. For example, it is said that the oldest wooden object inside the Cathedral, Prior Castell's clock in the south transept, was the only wooden object not burned by the Scottish prisoners of 1650 because of the Scottish thistle that it proudly displays above its face. While it is true that the clock is now the oldest wooden object in the Cathedral, there is also firm evidence to show that it had been dismantled and removed from the Cathedral prior to the time of the internment of the Scottish prisoners. It was not reinstalled until long after they had gone. Furthermore, the Cathedral woodwork was probably burned not by Scottish prisoners, but by the victorious Scottish army that took Durham in 1640 and used the Cathedral as a barracks.

The Cathedral from a train approaching Durham Station

Whatever the darker aspects of this cathedral and its history and mythology, I have only grown to love the place more and more. Having seen it first as a visitor, I have come to know it as a part of the daily landscape. Towering as it does above the city, it is hard to go anywhere in the city without seeing it several times each day – often from afar, and not infrequently from close up and within. Just walking past, on Palace Green, or walking through on my way to the Cathedral bookshop or as a short cut on my way home, I find myself again and again feeling hugely grateful for the opportunity to live so near to this beautiful and holy place.

Holy Places and their Stories

Holy places, however holy they may be, are still 'places'. That is, they are particular rather than general, and they are located in material space, rather than being ethereal (although I shall extend the concept at times to refer to mental space as well as geographical space). This book, therefore, takes a particular holy place – Durham Cathedral – as an example to work with. This will make this book different in some important ways to books that might have been written taking other holy places as their example. However, it will keep us linked to the tangible particularity that all holy places have in common. To talk of holy space in a general and abstract sense would not be at all the same kind of discussion.

Although other faith traditions have their own holy places (e.g. Mecca for Islam or Amritsar for Sikhs), and although Protestant Christians have traditionally had reservations about topics such as pilgrimage or shrines, I think that it is characteristically Christian to acknowledge this particularity and materiality of holy places. The incarnation of Christ is so central and important to Christianity, that we should be wary of any abstract holiness which is not located in the earthy reality of this world, with all its challenges and limitations. Just as Christian understandings of God require us to talk particularly of Jesus of Nazareth, so any Christian understanding of holy places will require us to keep our feet firmly on the ground – even though the limitations of this perspective will always remind us of the contrast between imperfect finite humanity and the holy infinity of God.

Human encounters with holy places will therefore also each have their own particularity, their own stories, anchored in the lives of the men and women who have found these places. That is not to say that there will be nothing that these stories will have in common, but rather that what they have in common will be a numinous holiness that is completely ineffable unless it finds expression in the particular stories of the places and people concerned. And, because people are human and imperfect, these stories will therefore almost inevitably each have their 'dark side', that aspect which reflects things which are not at all holy, but through which holiness is somehow nonetheless also communicated.

Perhaps the supreme example of all of this is to be found in the holy places in Jerusalem, where Jesus was crucified. The dark side of this story, and of this place, hardly needs any explanation. The gospel writers literally refer to a darkness coming upon the earth in association with the events that took place here.[1] The place was known as 'the place of the skull'.[2] It was a place of death and tears. Yet, such was the transforming power of faith in the subsequent resurrection of Christ that the day on which these events took place became known as 'Good' Friday, and the cross (an instrument of execution) became known among Christians as something that was 'holy'. So, the collect for Holy Cross Day takes the darkness of Christ's suffering as a basis for prayer for the transformation of our own suffering:

> Almighty God,
> who in the passion of your blessed Son
> made an instrument of painful death
> to be for us the means of life and peace:
> grant us so to glory in the cross of Christ
> that we may gladly suffer for his sake;
> who is alive and reigns with you,
> in the unity of the Holy Spirit,
> one God, now and for ever.
> Amen.[3]

Encounters with holy places can be costly. They invite us to suffer, not for suffering's sake, but for Christ's sake. They draw us into human darkness as a place of holy transformation.

Human stories, including the stories of the life of Jesus, are not only located in geographical and material space but also in time. They therefore typically have a development. An initial encounter with holiness has its impact upon us, but it must then be given time to reveal the depth of that impact. Will the holiness that we have encountered become a part of us, or will it quickly be forgotten? How will it affect our lives? How will it help us in the process of finding God in prayer afterwards? It is this need for temporal perspective that often leads to the metaphor of all Christian life as being a journey or pilgrimage. Journeys take us from place to place, and each new place (at least potentially) changes us along the way.

Journeys are a recurring theme in the early spirituality which preceded the Roman Catholic tradition in England, Ireland, Scotland and Wales, a spirituality which we will encounter again and again in this book. They are the subject of prayers such as this one:

The path I walk, Christ walks it. May the land in which I am be without sorrow.
May the Trinity protect me wherever I stay; Father, Son, and Holy Spirit.
Bright angels walk with me – dear presence – in every dealing.
In every dealing I pray them that no one's poison may reach me.
The ninefold people of heaven of holy cloud, the tenth force of the stout earth.
Favorable company, they come with me, so that the Lord may not be angry with me.
May I arrive at every place, may I return home; may the way in which I spend be a way without loss.
May every path before me be smooth, man, woman, and child welcome me.
A truly good journey! Well does the fair Lord show us a course, a path.[4]

This prayer, which probably originally referred to the journey through each day, reminds us that every journey on earth finds us in the company of Christ, of the Holy Trinity, of angelic beings ('the ninefold people of heaven')[5] and of the whole Church ('the tenth force').

Finding God in Durham Cathedral

Durham Cathedral has become for me a familiar place of prayer. Intimate celebrations of the Eucharist at a weekday lunchtime service, the larger congregation of Sunday Matins, and the very much larger congregations gathered for major festivals each have their own particular sense of the presence of Christ in our midst, and each invites a participation in the ongoing offering of prayers that has been made here for almost a thousand years. When life feels painful and space is needed to stop and take stock, the Cathedral has provided a place to retreat to for a few minutes or more, to be still, to pray and to reflect. Whatever the occasion, it is as though this building is a huge icon, a window into an eternal reality in which those of us who are still alive on earth can join with the whole company of heaven in prayer. Somehow, the building invites prayer, it beckons us to come forward and to become a part of something greater than ourselves. It invites us to kneel down and recall how small and ephemeral a part of this world we each individually are.

I am sure that many others could give their own accounts of how this building has encouraged them to pray and of what it has meant to them in their prayers. I have watched as pilgrims have placed candles on Cuthbert's tomb, as visitors have sat in silence to absorb the atmosphere, and as sometimes huge congregations have gathered together here. I have been moved by those who kneel alone in solitude to share their inmost thoughts and concerns with God. I have been puzzled by those who pass through so quickly, and apparently carelessly and prayerlessly. But, unlike the huge building to which these diverse souls are visibly attracted, silent prayers are not visible to human eyes. God alone can see what is in the heart, both of the pilgrim who appears devout, as well as the visitor who apparently does not care.

Alongside the moving experiences of seeing the Cathedral full of students, of seeing Advent candles processed down the nave in darkness, of being present at Midnight Mass on Christmas Eve, of gathering around the fire in the cloister at dawn on Easter morning, and other special occasions, including especially my daughter's wedding, the opportunities to participate in the life of the Cathedral that I have most appreciated have been in and around Morning Prayer. This has provided for me a rhythm and regularity about which the Benedictine founders of the Cathedral would doubtless have felt that I still have much to learn. However, like them, I have found that recitation of the psalms encompasses much, if not all, of that which needs to be said in prayer. Like them, I have found that I need to listen to scripture each day and somehow turn it into my own prayer. Like them, I have found that work and study need to fit around this priority of prayer rather than the other way around. Unlike them, of course, I still have a long way to go in getting the balance right – but then even the Benedictine rule was explicitly offered only as a beginning, and like them I have had to start somewhere.

So, where should my reflections on praying in this holy place begin? They are primarily reflections on experiences of a place of prayer, and so I have begun with a story of how I first encountered that place and my impressions of it. The place about which I am writing is, however, in many ways not so much a building as a personal place, a place of prayer that is not so easily fixed in time or space, except insofar as it is fixed in the 'place' of my own experience. And so perhaps I should have begun with a more autobiographical account of my own beginnings in prayer, my first encounters of this place. I could, for example, have begun with my own experiences of learning to pray as a child. Or, perhaps, I could have begun with people whom I have met and whose books I have read through whom I have been introduced to the beauty, desolation, peace and mystery that constitute the place of prayer. These memories, experiences and places of prayer are 'inner places', all of which influence the way in which we experience holy places in the outer world. I shall give more careful consideration to these in the next chapter. In various ways they influence our desire to find God.

Our search for God in holy places will ultimately be motivated by our desire to find him. Often we do not desire to find God as much as we would like to, and so this too needs to be a subject of our prayers:

O Lord our God,
grant us grace to desire you with our whole heart;
that so desiring, we may seek and find you;
and so finding, may love you;
and so loving, may hate those sins from which you have delivered us;
through Jesus Christ our Lord.
Amen.[6]

Starting Places

It is important to remember that the history of any holy place actually begins before we arrive at it, in the lives and experiences of other people who have been there before us. To think about that history first is not to turn the experience into an academic exercise (although there is always the danger of that) or to try to evade a personal encounter with God (although it could allow that too) but rather to recognize that the place has become what it is because of the encounters with God that other people have experienced there before us. It may help us to avoid an excessively individual or overly subjective approach to our prayers, and it reminds us that we pray as part of a Church that transcends time. To think in different ways about a holy place, and to explore it in all its different dimensions, is therefore helpful and appropriate if one is serious about finding God there. Or, if knowing God is really a love affair, it might be more like an insatiable desire for getting to know places and things connected with one's lover. Of course, it will not always be necessary, for unprepared people can and do encounter God in holy places. But if we are serious about actively searching for God, it seems to me that this might be a good place to start.

Getting to Know Durham Cathedral

Durham Cathedral is thought to be the third church to have been built on the site that it occupies on the sandstone peninsula that is at the heart of the city of Durham. The church that immediately preceded it, the so-called 'White Church', was built in 998 by the monks who, fleeing from Viking raiders, first brought St Cuthbert's body to Durham from Lindisfarne. Begun in 1093 by the first Prince Bishop, William of St Carileph, the present building was largely completed in only 40 years. From the twelfth to the fifteenth centuries, the western towers, the Galilee Chapel, the Chapel of the Nine Altars and the central tower were added. Despite this, and despite some rather destructive approaches to restoration in the eighteenth century,[7] it still retains its distinctive Norman character. It is built of sandstone quarried initially from just across the river (in the vicinity of what is now Quarry Heads Lane and Margery Lane) and later from Kepier, about a mile away along the River Wear, east of Durham. It was constructed on shallow foundations, directly upon the underlying sandstone of the Durham peninsula. It is 143 metres in length and the central tower is 67 metres high.

The presence of the earthly remains of St Cuthbert, St Bede, and other saints, determined from the start the nature and mission of the Christian community that prayed here, worked here and lived here. In the middle ages, Durham was one of the leading destinations for pilgrimage in Europe, competing in England primarily with Canterbury. The Chapel of the Nine Altars was built specifically to accommodate, and impress, the great number of pilgrims who came to Durham. This cathedral has therefore always been a destination for pilgrims who have come to visit the tombs of Cuthbert and Bede, or else to search for God, or to look for healing, or simply to wonder at a beautiful building. Today, people from all over the world still come to pray, to wonder, to look for God, or simply to satisfy their curiosity.

The presence of the tombs of Cuthbert and Bede is significant not just because of the way in which they shaped this holy place as a destination for pilgrims. They also represent a link with an early Christian tradition in northeast England, which preceded the Roman tradition that came to dominate following the Synod of Whitby in 664. The Synod of Whitby is traditionally said to have effected this transition to a primarily Roman tradition, a transition through which Cuthbert lived and which Bede documented. However, its significance in this regard is now debated and its concerns with such matters as the timing of Easter and the kind of tonsure imposed on monks appear strange to us. The Christian spirituality of the early English, Irish, Welsh and Scottish saints was tough, and knew an ascetic discipline (derived from the Desert Fathers of fourth century Egypt) which was harsher than most Christians today would even wish to imagine. Its spiritual and theological emphases, while not completely unique, were identifiably different in flavour to the Roman Christianity, which it encountered in the northeast corner of England at the point in history that interests us. They included, among other things, the importance of the quest for the transcendent, human life itself as a pilgrimage orientated towards this quest, and an understanding of the sacredness of place and time. It was a strongly incarnational tradition in its understanding of how the divine is encountered in a material world. These emphases are implicit more than explicit in Durham Cathedral, but evidence of them remains and they will be illustrated in this book by quotation from various sources. They are not entirely absent from Roman Christianity or its traditions of spirituality, which will also be quoted here, but they are differently emphasized and given expression in arguably characteristic ways.

Durham Cathedral was built at the heart of a monastic foundation in the Benedictine tradition. Life in the Benedictine order was, and still is, structured according to the Rule of St Benedict (c.480–c.547). At the heart of this life was a rhythm of work, study and prayer which revolved around seven fixed times for liturgical prayer each day. The rule also emphasizes humility, obedience and hospitality, but prayer was central to everything.

In addition to liturgical prayer, the practice of *lectio divina* became especially associated with the Benedictine tradition. *Lectio divina*, or literally 'divine reading', emphasizes reflection upon reading, and especially upon the reading of scripture. Guigo (d. 1188), a Carthusian monk, described four stages or 'moments' to this practice. First, the text is simply read, slowly and thoughtfully (*lectio*) and secondly its meaning and imagery are the focus of reflection (*meditatio*). Thirdly comes *oratio*, a prayerful response to what has been read, and finally comes *contemplatio*, or a silent contemplation which goes beyond words.

The Cathedral was also a base from which the mission of the Church could be pursued, and it was the place in which the seat of the bishop, the *cathedra*, was located. In the case of Durham Cathedral, it was the seat of a Prince Bishop who, until the nineteenth century, also exercised considerable powers on behalf of the crown. Its strategic and prominent location on the Durham peninsula was chosen for both its defensibility and its visibility. The visible presence of this cathedral in the landscape, which continues to impress visitors today, was always intended to be a sign and symbol of something invisible, an ambiguous mixture of divine and human power.

But if the Cathedral was symbolic of political power and justice it was also a place of safety for the marginalized and vulnerable. Until 1623, according to the right of sanctuary, fugitives who grasped the sanctuary knocker on the north door[8] would be offered refuge for 37 days, after which they would either have to leave the country or face trial. Women, who were initially excluded from Cuthbert's shrine, were made welcome in the Galilee Chapel. The poor who were sick were cared for by the monastic community, at nearby Kepier Hospital.

Durham Cathedral was an outstanding architectural project of its time, and the relatively limited changes that have been made to it since its original construction make it one of the best remaining examples of Norman architecture in Europe. It was built by invading political masters who wished to acquire by association the authority of a saint who had long preceded them, and also to emphasize their own authority to rule. However, the craftsmanship and political motivation of the pro-

ject can never entirely eclipse the primary motivation of the builders of this great building that it should be a place in which people might pray and thus encounter God. It was built as a holy place, within which God might be found.

Like most Christian churches prior to the Reformation, Durham Cathedral was built so that its plan was in the shape of a cross. All of the parts of the Cathedral which are focused on in this book are to be found on the upright vertical section of that cross, in other words on its east to west axis. However, the reader who wants to explore this holy place properly will not

The replica of the original sanctuary knocker on the North Door

neglect the north and south transepts, which form the arm of the cross, or the neighbouring buildings of the pre-Reformation monastery: the Chapter House, the Prior's Hall, the great kitchen, the monks' dormitory and the cloister around which they were built.[9]

The Cathedral Church of Christ, Blessed Mary the Virgin and St Cuthbert of Durham[10] today continues to provide a place of pilgrimage and prayer, a seat for the Bishop of Durham, and a focus for the mission of the Church within the Diocese of Durham and the Church of England. It is no longer the home of a monastic community, for this was dissolved by Henry VIII on 31 December 1539. However, it is the home of a praying Christian community in Durham, it continues to be a sign of a Christian presence in Durham, and is actively engaged with the wider community of the region.

According to its website,[11] the Cathedral aims to:

- 'be a sign of the presence of God in the world as sacred space and through the daily offering of praise and prayer
- live out the meaning of Christian community as a place of hospitality and sanctuary
- bear witness to the gospel through evangelism, service, environmental and social responsibility and by practical care for those in need
- encourage and support pilgrimage and spiritual formation
- provide a focus for adult and children's Christian education, and for theological reflection and intellectual engagement in the region in partnership with the University and Diocese of Durham
- support the mission of the Bishop and Diocese of Durham, and to collaborate ecumenically with the churches of the region
- conserve and develop the fabric and historic artefacts of the Cathedral and its ancillary buildings as part of a World Heritage Site, and to interpret its significance to visitors
- celebrate and promote human creativity through music and the arts
- promote the welfare of the city, the county and the north-east region in partnership with other religious and secular agencies.'

The Cathedral is not only a place of prayer, pilgrimage and Christian mission, but a destination for tourists and school parties, a focus of the annual miners' gala, a world heritage site, and the place in which Durham University degrees are conferred by the Chancellor of the University (a university which was founded in 1832 by the then Bishop of Durham and Cathedral Chapter), to name but a few of its roles in the community. This context is a helpful reminder that the Cathedral is not so much a quiet place in which Christians may retreat from the world (although it certainly can be this) but is rather a place in which God, the Church and the wider community come into engagement with one another.

The Cloisters

Most of this book will be about themes that arise from an encounter with the interior of Durham Cathedral. If it were about an outdoor holy place (for example, the Holy Island of Lindisfarne) I think that many similar themes would arise, but perhaps also some different ones. I will therefore consider here briefly just one part of the Cathedral that might qualify as being out of doors.

The cloisters were not originally an outdoor place. Although today they are open to the central square that they define, they were originally fitted with stained glass windows. It might still be argued that they have always been 'out of doors', being endowed with major doorways to allow ingress and egress at each of their four corners, not to mention other doors leading to the Chapter House, Priory, monks' dormitory, refectory and library. Indeed these doors provide an important part of the character of the cloisters. They are at once an access and an exit to the Cathedral. They also connect the Cathedral to other parts of the monastic complex. They are thus a major thoroughfare and people are almost constantly coming and going through them.

The word 'cloister', meaning in this case a 'covered walk', also has a sense of seclusion, and can be used to refer to a monastery or monastic life. This sense is also a very important part of the character of the cloisters at Durham, and elsewhere. They are a secluded place, even when filled with noisy school children or other visitors enjoying a packed lunch. They are apart from the world, but they are also apart from the Cathedral. They are at once connected to the wider world, but also set apart from it.

This secluded openness is reflected in the function of the cloisters. They would originally have been used for washing (at the stone basin in the centre), exercise, study and learning, writing, and quiet meditation. So it is today. People come and go to work, clergy come and go from services in the Cathedral, and staff and visitors come and go from the shop, restaurant, library and treasury. This is a place which draws together much of what will be encountered elsewhere in the Cathedral: the daily routine, work and leisure, community and solitude, thoughtfulness and contemplation.

For all that is going on here, and the distractions that these activities bring, this is still a holy place in which God may be found. It is possible to walk around it quietly (or amidst the hubbub of daily comings and goings) and find that it draws thoughts towards prayer. The rhythm of walking around it can act like the repetitions of a rosary, or of the Jesus prayer. Each step taken can be a prayer of desire to draw closer to God. Each entry into the cloisters is a drawing aside for prayer. Each exit (unless going into the Cathedral to pray) is a return to the wider world where our prayers may be put to the test of daily life. In between each arrival and each departure, the cloisters provide a place to reflect, to read, to rest or to pray.

Remembering that the Cathedral treasury is to be found in the southwest corner of the cloisters, it may be appropriate to finish this section with the prayer of a local hermit, Godric of Finchale (c.1065–1170), who drew aside from a busy life as a merchant in order to spend time in prayer:

> Lord Jesus you know that I have no other treasure on this earth than you, and you only, my God and Lord.[12]

Finding a Holy Place

We might encounter holy places unexpectedly, as I did Durham Cathedral, or else, like pilgrims, we might go looking for them. Wherever and however we find them, they are signposts to God. Like other signposts, we can ignore them if we wish. We can decide that they point to places that were not on the route that we had planned for our journey, and we can continue on our way. We might decide to come back to them another day, or we can decide that this is a turning that we never wish to take. Or else, excited by what they promise, we can abandon our other plans and follow them come what may. Our decisions will doubtless reflect many things about ourselves and about the particular 'signpost', or holy place, that we have found. They may be intuitive, whether out of love and enthusiasm or suspicion and distrust, or they may be analytically made and reflected upon at length. In every case, they can lead us closer to finding God, or they can take us away from him. They are therefore worth thinking about carefully.

Durham Cathedral is a good example with which to work in this book, because it is so rich in images, symbols, associations, history, atmosphere and spirituality, and because it offers something that will appeal widely to people of differing types. However, because it is a signpost to us on an inner journey, as well as a journey that leads us beyond ourselves, it will lead us (if we allow it to) to examine ourselves as a necessary part of the process of finding God. A recurring theme of this book will be the way in which inner and outer places point to each other and together help us in our prayers. It will largely be about the way in which outer places (holy places in a literal, spatial and geographical, sense) point us to inner (emotional, thoughtful and spiritual) places. However, we must not forget that we will also all find holy places within ourselves that provide pointers for exploring the physical world around us. If holy places are places in which we find God, we must be ready to find him deep within ourselves as well as in the world around us.

We have seen that sacraments, pilgrimage, refuge, liturgical and contemplative prayer, and pilgrimage are all aspects of the life and history of Durham Cathedral. As I have prayed in different parts of the Cathedral, as I have responded to the invitation to pray that this holy place has seemed to offer me, I have found that these themes are still to be encountered, almost as though they are embedded in the very fabric of the place. Different chapters of this book will focus on each of these themes in turn, although they are by no means intended to be exclusive or comprehensive. Before tackling these themes, however, we shall turn in the next chapter to some general reflections on finding God in a holy place, and some of the ways in which they relate to the inner places of our hearts and minds. Before moving on to do that, you may like to pause and spend some time exploring holy places of your own.

◈

Exploring Holy Places

Places of prayer sometimes take us by surprise, but if we are seriously seeking God we will also find ourselves searching out new places and revisiting those that we know well. They may be places in our hearts and minds, or places in time, or in geographical space. Each chapter of this book will conclude with invitations to explore prayer in Durham Cathedral or in other places. This chapter concludes with some suggested ways in which to prepare for a pilgrimage to Durham Cathedral, or to some other holy place, or as a way of preparing to explore new places of prayer in the future.

Exploring Durham Cathedral

The question to be addressed when planning a pilgrimage to Durham Cathedral, or elsewhere, is how to balance being a tourist with being a pilgrim. These are certainly not mutually exclusive ways of visiting, but each can easily eclipse the other given a chance. Within holy places, time needs to be given to take in one's surroundings and it can help to allow time to do some fact finding before making space specifically for prayer.

You might like to read this book through before making a visit to Durham Cathedral or (if you are staying in Durham for a few days) you might like to read a new chapter before each of a series of shorter visits. There are also good guidebooks and other resources to be obtained from the Cathedral shop which provide further information about the history, art and architecture of the Cathedral. Guided tours are taken regularly during the tourist season, and the Cathedral offers organized pilgrimages for groups who request this. It may even be helpful to make an initial exploratory visit as a tourist and then to return later with the specific purpose of prayer. However, a very good way to start might be to make a pilgrim visit using the guide written for this purpose by the Dean of Durham.[13]

Having made your initial visit, find space to reflect quietly on what you found. Perhaps it would be helpful to allow time for a few minutes sitting outside after your visit (if the weather is fine) or in the cloisters, or after returning home or to your room, or before bedtime that day. What parts of the Cathedral most left an impression on you? What fact most interested you? What symbols did you notice? How did the Cathedral make you feel, and how do you feel now? What did you learn about God? What did you learn about yourself?

God of love and truth and beauty, for whose praise this house of prayer was built: open our eyes to glimpse your beauty; open our minds to grasp your truth; and open our hearts to welcome that great love with which, in Jesus Christ, you love your world. We ask this for his sake. Amen.[14]

Exploring New Places

What new places would you like to explore in prayer? Again, you might like to consider answers to this question metaphorically and literally. Think widely and imaginatively. Consider possible places that you would like to go which might seem unrealistic, as well as those that you could actually choose to visit. If you feel that you need some new ideas, hopefully you will find some of the ideas suggested later in this book to be helpful. You may also like to read more widely about different approaches to prayer.[15]

Once you have spent a little time on this, identify two or three particular places that you would like to visit. Find out more about these places and make some plans to actually visit one of them. For example:

- Identify within your daily routine one or two places that could become new places of prayer and think about ways in which you can realistically ensure that you do visit at least one of these places every day. For example, you might decide to set the alarm clock earlier, to create a new place of prayer before leaving home or beginning your household chores each day. Or you might identify time on the train to work, or at lunchtime, when you could read a short passage of scripture. Even mundane tasks such as filling the car with petrol, or collecting cash from the cash-point machine, can become new places for prayer. Be imaginative and be realistic!
- Alternatively, you might like to identify new places in which you can continue your existing pattern of prayer. For example, perhaps a different time would work better, or a different room?
- Find out about a new place that belongs to a particular tradition – e.g. the Ignatian, Carmelite or Benedictine traditions. There are many good books available to help with exploring new places of this kind.[16] If possible, find a Spiritual Director who can guide you in exploring this new place of prayer.
- You may like to identify geographical places that you would like to visit on retreat or pilgrimage. If you have a particular place in mind in which you want to undertake these explorations, then it might be helpful to find out at least a little more about it before you make your visit. It can be very frustrating to return home only to discover that you missed something of key significance while you were there! If you want your time there to allow space for prayer, it can be helpful to have done some of the fact finding in advance.

In preparation for your exploration of these new places, you may like to undertake a *lectio divina* using the following verses from the book of Jeremiah:

> For surely I know the plans I have for you, says the Lord, plans for your welfare and not for harm, to give you a future with hope. Then when you call upon me and come and pray to me, I will

hear you. When you search for me, you will find me; if you seek me with all your heart, I will let you find me, says the LORD . . .[17]

Follow the pattern outlined earlier:

1. *Read* the verses through slowly, at least two or three times, so as to become familiar with them.
2. *Meditate* on their meaning; ask yourself questions about this passage and search for the truth within it.
3. *Pray* about what you have read and reflected on, and your response to it.
4. *Contemplate* – in silence and without words – that you are in God's presence and that he is with you.

Chapter 2

Finding God in a Holy Place

'But will God indeed reside with mortals on earth? Even heaven and the highest heaven cannot contain you, how much less this house that I have built!'[1]

Finding God

How can we find God? This question seems to me to be what prayer is all about, and yet it presents a huge paradox. Something of the same paradox is found in the words of Solomon, as recorded in the second book of Chronicles, on the occasion of the dedication of the first Hebrew Temple in Jerusalem. The transcendence of God, as understood in the Hebrew and Christian traditions, is such that it is impossible to imagine God 'residing' on earth alongside human beings at all. Far less could a particular building, however beautiful and magnificent, ever 'contain' God. Even the heavens, including all that we now know of space and the universe, cannot contain God. If anything, it is all the other way around. 'In him we live and move and have our being.'[2] We are somehow to be found 'in' God. But God cannot be found 'in' our world – except insofar as he is to be found everywhere.

If God is to be found everywhere, then surely there shouldn't be any problem? After all, it is also fundamental to the Christian tradition that God is immanent, as well as transcendent. Immanence speaks of finding God wherever he is sought, of his pervading of all things, of his presence in intimate closeness with everything that exists. Immanence is a feature of many of the world's major faith traditions, not just Christianity, but it is especially important for Christians because we believe that God made himself present with us in Christ in a very particular way. Because of this historical 'making present', this revelation of God in Christ, Christians understand God as continuing to be present, and continuing to reveal himself in the material order of things today.

So, to return to our original question, 'How can we find God?' The answer seems simple. He is everywhere. In fact, as the psalmist reminds us, it is impossible to escape from him:

> If I ascend to heaven, you are there; if I make my bed in Sheol, you are there. If I take the wings of the morning and settle at the farthest limits of the sea, even there your hand shall lead me, and your right hand shall hold me fast. If I say, "Surely the darkness shall cover me, and the light around me become night," even the darkness is not dark to you; the night is as bright as the day, for darkness is as light to you.[3]

We don't have to 'find' God at all, rather everything is 'found' within God. But herein lies the paradox. Even though God is everywhere, even though he is continuously and universally present, human beings still have a sense of needing to find him. Even if at some intellectual level, or as an act of faith, we acknowledge that he is present, it often feels very much like he isn't. The darkness may not be dark to God, but it can still seem very dark to us.

There may be various senses in which this darkness is actually characteristic of all of life in this world. So, for example, the author of the *Cloud of Unknowing* reminds us that God is so much infinitely greater than anything that we can see or know that we must 'unknow' everything in order to find him. As this unknowing is completely the opposite of all that we know in this world, this world must be characterized by a more or less continuous not knowing the presence of God. This negative, or 'apophatic', theology emphasizes the unknowability of an infinite God by finite creatures.

Positive (or 'cataphatic') Christian theology emphasizes ongoing human separation from God. Because God is holy, we are continuously separated from him in this world by our 'sin', by our failure to live perfect and holy lives. In the early chapters of the book of Genesis human beings are first portrayed as living in close proximity to God. However, following their disobedience they hide from God in shame and are then excluded by God from the garden of his presence as punishment.

These pervasive senses of the unknowability of God, or of human separation from God, must be balanced by the emphasis that the incarnation of Christ places upon the presence of God with us. They are only one half of the paradox; they are not the full truth. God is present always and everywhere in this world – even though there are ways in which he will always seem absent.

However, there are other ways in which God seems more or less present in different ways, at different times and in different places. Even if we turn to the gospel accounts of the birth, life, death and resurrection of Jesus, we should be challenged by the ways in which God seems intimately present at some times – as at the baptism of Jesus or in the accounts of the healing miracles – and then painfully absent at other times – most notably at the crucifixion. And we must not forget that almost 30 years of Jesus' life is unknown to us. If remarkable things happened during those years, they did not prevent members of Jesus' own community from seeing him as a very ordinary figure – a carpenter's son.[4] If God was continuously present in Christ, as Christians believe, then he certainly didn't always *seem* to be present.

When we look at our own lives in today's world, the varying sense of the presence and absence of God is even more marked. Standing on a hilltop watching a beautiful sunset, or finding healing from sickness in response to prayer, or moved by worship amidst a lively and responsive congregation, it can be very easy to know that God is present. Catching a train at 6.30 a.m. to travel to work on a Monday morning, feeling hurt by the thoughtless comments of a fellow Christian, or standing by the bedside of someone whom you love deeply who has just died, it can all feel very different.

Perhaps relationship with God is rather like marriage. We can have moments of feeling deeply in love, but we can also have times of feeling far apart, and much of life is lived somewhere in between. Married life has its highs and lows but much of it is very ordinary. Not that God's love for us ever changes, but our feelings for and about him certainly do. It is this psychological fluctuation in our feelings about God that presents us with the challenge of finding God in prayer. If Christian faith is worth anything, it should seek God in Christ in all things: in experiences of crucifixion as well as those of resurrection, and in the ordinary as well as the extraordinary experiences of life. But how do we do that?

It seems to me that there are times, people, places and experiences that seem to bring us 'close' to God. Of course, we can't always live in a sense of closeness to God, or at least most of us don't, but perhaps there are things that we can learn from the times and places that seem to bring us close to God, which will help us in other times and places?

This is not to say that feelings of closeness to God are necessarily everything. Perhaps we will feel close to God and be deceived. The most awful things have sometimes been done by people who thought they were close to God. On the other hand, perhaps we will feel far away from God and actually be very close. We must not forget that Jesus' cry of dereliction on the cross: 'My God, my God, why have you forsaken me?'[5], was uttered at the climax of his obedience to his heavenly father. If this was indicative of how he felt as a human being at that moment in time, then those who follow him can hardly expect things to be any easier. However, even if feelings can be misleading, they are still important and must not be completely ignored. It would certainly be sad if we never felt close to God, and it is certainly painful when God feels far away.

What is being suggested here, then, is not that we must be ruled by our feelings, or that we must always expect to feel close to God. Rather, we must be realistic. God will sometimes feel far away. But perhaps the key to coping with these experiences of feeling deserted by God is to be found in our other experiences of feeling close to God. And perhaps, during these more intimate experiences of the presence of God, we can establish a relationship with him that will sustain us in times of dereliction. Jesus remained faithful to God, his father, in a time and place of the most awful sense of the absence of God. Surely this was only possible because of the sense of intimacy with God as father that had been so characteristic of much, if not all, of the preceding years of his life?

The broader implications of all of this are that we must establish a relationship of intimacy with God in prayer that is a part of the very fabric of our lives if we are to remain faithful to God at the times when he seems most distant. This concerns our self-discipline in exploring, establishing and maintaining patterns of prayer. It concerns our understanding of what it means to be followers of Christ. It concerns our understanding of how a loving and omnipotent God relates to us in a world that is, at once, full of so much beauty and so much pain. It concerns our understanding of what it means to be human beings: time-bound creatures with body, mind and spirit. This book will not attempt to explore thoroughly all of these questions. Rather, it is a book about just one aspect of all of this: How can we take beautiful times and places and use them to sustain our faith in difficult times and places?

If we are adults, or even children, with some years of experience of relating to God, a little reflection should suffice to remind us that certain times and places have tended to leave us with a sense of being closer to God. The purpose of this book is to explore ways in which we can make use of that kind of knowledge of ourselves and of God's world in such a way as to build on the sense of closeness to God that those times and places have brought us. This building is not undertaken simply that we might *feel* close to God, but rather that we might be better equipped for times when we do not feel close to God. In other words, it is undertaken in order that we might build lives that *are* close to the life of God in Christ however we might feel.

The specific example that is explored here is one of a building as a place in which God might be found. Of course, a building cannot 'contain' God – the very notion is absurd. We must also, therefore, be very careful that we do not allow such a thing to become limiting or to give us too small a picture of what God is like. However, if we do find that there are some places in which we 'find' God, then perhaps a little bit of further thought about, and exploration of, those places might help us to build a better picture of what God is really like and thus, in some sense, to know him better.

Holy Places

Holy places can take many forms. The word 'place' is being used here largely in the sense that there are particular geographical, architectural, or other literal places in which we feel close to God. However, there are also metaphorical 'places' in our lives where we meet with God: emotional places, sacramental places, places which provide a turning point or transition, places of loss – or achievement, places to which we are led in thought, places of decision and many other such places. These are not always easy places in which to be, but they are characterized by a sense of the nearness of God. Perhaps the archetype of both kinds of place might be found in Jacob's place of encounter with God in his dreams.

Having cheated his brother, Esau, of his birthright, Jacob was hated by Esau, and Esau planned to kill him. Jacob therefore fled. Whilst on his way to his uncle's house, he found himself one day, after sunset, in a 'certain place'.[6] Resting his head on a stone for a pillow he fell asleep. He dreamed of a ladder, with its top in heaven, and with angels ascending and descending on it. The text tells us that, God 'stood beside' Jacob in his dream, and that he blessed him, promising him both the land on which he slept and also offspring so numerous that they would spread to the ends of the earth. When Jacob awoke, he said:

Surely the Lord is in this place – and I did not know it!' And he was afraid, and said, 'How awesome is this place! This is none other than the house of God, and this is the gate of heaven.[7]

This dream is important in both the Hebrew and Christian traditions, for the latter not least because of the words of Jesus in Jn 1.51, taken to indicate an understanding of the ladder between earth and heaven as symbolic of Christ. However, it seems to me that this story also recognizes that places can be important.

Like Jacob, we can find that some places – both literal and metaphorical places – can be places of encounter with God. God tells Jacob in his dream that he will be with him and will keep him wherever he goes. But this place, a place that Jacob names Bethel – 'House of God', is still special. It is a place to remember; it is more than merely symbolic, it is a sacramental place. It is not an entirely easy place to be in. Jacob is afraid. But it is a place of being blessed; it is a gateway into heaven.

This experience, this place, took Jacob by surprise. Such experiences, such places, cannot be engineered. They are stumbled across, by the grace of God, when and where God wills. There are other places, however, places that are also gateways into heaven, which we can visit and revisit and, of course, even Bethel was a place that was open to being revisited. These places might be places of relationship, as when a particular spiritual director, friend or mentor provides a place of encounter with God. They might be sacramental places, particularly the place of the Eucharist. They might be places in scripture. They might be places of prayer, offered perhaps by a daily routine that makes space for God. Or they might be special places provided by a building, by an icon, or by a place in the countryside.

Recognising Holy Places

A holy place is a place that becomes a 'gateway to heaven', a place in which we are aware of the presence of God, a place in which in some special sense we 'find' God. Places with this kind of quality, as has already been said, may be very varied. How, then, will we know when we have found one?

The obvious answer to this question is that, if we have not been aware of the presence of God, the place in which we have been was not such a place. But what does it mean to be aware of the presence of God? After all, God cannot usually be seen or heard in any literal sense. So what does it mean to say that we are aware of the presence of God?

Awareness of God comes to us in different ways. In particular, I think that we become aware of God through symbols, sacraments, events and memories. Let's consider each of these in turn.

Symbols enable us to make associations of meaning with particular things that we sense or experience more directly. So, for example, a beautiful sunset might evoke within us a sense of gratitude towards the creator of the natural order around us. Or a painting of the crucifixion might evoke a new appreciation of God's sharing of human suffering in Christ. Or perhaps the scale and stillness of a cathedral nave might induce within us a sense of wonder and awe at the immensity and timelessness of God. Incense, icons, music, and movement in liturgy can all work in a similar way. In all of these ways, and in many other ways, more or less conscious and rational associations lead us from things that we can see and hear and touch (and taste and smell) to an awareness of the God whom we cannot physically sense, but who communicates his presence to us through any or all of our senses. They offer us pictures of God – or at least they help us to paint such pictures in our minds.

Of a similar order are the letters and words that form language. These are really only symbols too, but they are capable of conveying very precise, varied and subtle meaning. We can develop awareness of God by reading about him – in scripture, in spiritual writings, in biography, in theological works and in many other genres of literature. This, of course, is always likely to be a conscious and rational process, although allegorical stories and hidden meanings might evoke associations with God that might be neither fully conscious nor fully rational. Either way, some places might become holy for us because of the information that has come to us through reading or hearing about them. So, for example, a sense of the presence of God while visiting a place of pilgrimage might be generated by all that we have read about that place or about the experiences of encounter with God that others have had in that place.

A particular awareness of God may also come to us through the sacraments. These are symbols, especially of the body and blood of Christ at the Eucharist, and of new life at baptism. For Catholic Christians sacraments will always be more than merely symbols, and there is no doubt that the words, actions and liturgy of the Eucharist will always put this sacrament in a special place of its own in its capacity to represent, evoke and engage a sense of the presence of Christ.

We may also interpret other events as indicative of the presence of God. The birth of a baby, the death of someone we love, an act of kindness, or a 'coincidence' with particular significance, may all cause us to sense the presence and agency of God. These events, and the collective or individual memory of them, might then confer a sense of holiness on a particular place – as, for example, at the site of Thomas Becket's death in Canterbury Cathedral.

Symbols and sacraments, events and memories, then, provide various ways in which we become aware of the presence of God – of the Holy – in particular places, and at particular times. All of these can help us to find God, as long as the rational element of these experiences is not distorted in such a way that we then diminish or deny their significance. These things are also predictable, and might help us to identify places that hold particular significance for us as holy places – places where we might expect to find an especial awareness of God.

According to Rudolf Otto,[8] however, the Holy may also be experienced in a unique, direct and non-rational way. Although he considered such experiences (which he termed 'numinous') to be largely ineffable, he nonetheless identified two aspects of these direct experiences of the Holy. First, they are associated with a sense of awe, majesty or power: which he referred to as the *mysterium tremendum*. Secondly, they are associated with a sense of desire; they are seductive and fascinating. This he referred to as the *mysterium fascinans*. It is a natural human capacity to have such experiences but it is not possible to convey in words what a numinous experience is like: they are quite unlike any other experiences that human beings might have.

It will not be possible to predict when and where we might experience the numinous, except that perhaps we might identify particular places in which we have had, or are more likely to have, numinous experiences. So, for example, we might find that we often experience an awareness of the numinous in the countryside, or on a mountaintop. We might experience the numinous during the Eucharist, or even in the context of a sexual relationship (although, in the latter case, there are also other powerful physical and psychological processes going on which might be easily confused with the numinous). We might also have memories of such experiences in a particular place, which might make it a place to which we want to return. The numinous may therefore be experienced in symbols, sacraments, events, and in memories, but it is not necessarily confined to these contexts.

The *mysterium tremendum* may not always be something that we are in a hurry to encounter, and places in which we have such experiences might therefore also make us afraid. Holy places may, sometimes, be places that we feel we want to avoid. In such cases, the question will arise as to whether our desire for God as *mysterium fascinans* matches or exceeds our fear of God as *mysterium tremendum* and perhaps some places may have more of an association with one than with the other.

We may know that we have found a holy place, then, when by rational or non-rational means we become aware of the presence of

God there. To the extent that there is a rational component to this, we may be able to find holy places through deliberate searching or mental reflection. To the extent that the process is non-rational, we may find that such holiness takes us by surprise. However, once we have been surprised by the numinous, we may find that a return to the place of that encounter may be helpful in our search for God in both rational and non-rational ways.

Praying in Holy Places

What should we do if we find ourselves in a holy place? I am reluctant to lay down any rules here, for I think that responses to the holy have to be personal and sincere. That which comes naturally and intuitively, is most likely to be the right thing to do – at least in this context. However, a few things might be said that could perhaps be helpful.

Firstly, we shouldn't treat such places lightly. Even if God is everywhere, the holiness of the particular place arises because of its association with the presence of God. To behave in an over-familiar, or casual, way might therefore suggest that we have not recognized the awe-fullness of the *mysterium tremendum*, or that our picture of God is limited, unbalanced or simply far too small. Examples of encounters with holy places in scripture tend to support the idea that we should treat such places with respect as a means of communicating respect for God himself. We have already looked at the example of Jacob at Bethel. His response was to erect the stone that he had formerly used as a pillow to become a monument, and to make a vow to God. Amongst other examples we might consider Moses. When he encountered the burning bush, he heard the voice of God saying to him:

> Come no closer! Remove the sandals from your feet, for the place on which you are standing is holy ground.[9]

We are left to assume that Moses was obedient to this command, but we are left in no doubt of the impact that the encounter had upon him:

> Moses hid his face, for he was afraid to look at God.[10]

For most of us, removing our shoes might not seem to be a helpful thing to do, although we should note that in the Islamic tradition, this is still an obligation today when entering a mosque. I can see no reason at all why Christians shouldn't show respect for God in the same way, except perhaps that our self-consciousness at doing this, and the strangeness of the action, could easily become a distraction from prayer rather than an aid to prayer. Hiding our faces might come more naturally, and we talk of 'hiding our faces in shame' as a figure of speech. But the task here is not so much to copy exact biblical actions (even though this might sometimes be very helpful) as to find actions which are culturally and personally appropriate to our encounter with God; both as *mysterium tremendens* and *mysterium fascinans*. Just as places communicate holiness by symbolism and association, so our actions can communicate our reverence, submission and awe in response to that which is holy.

What might be appropriate by way of response on one occasion might well not be appropriate on the next, and we therefore also need to be wary of expecting that, if we do the same kinds of things in the same place, God will respond to order. This is especially true, perhaps, if we have had a very emotional encounter with God – as for example if we have been moved to tears. Such an experience should not lead us to imagine that every encounter with God will be marked in this way, or that tears should become the immediate objective when finding oneself in prayer in a holy place. We need, rather, to learn to encounter God in a variety of ways. We need to be patient, and to allow God to make us aware of his presence in different and varied and unexpected ways.

The number of responses that might be offered in the presence of the holy is enormous, and self-consciousness about doing the 'right' thing is unlikely to be helpful. Opposite and diverse responses may be equally appropriate for different people or on different occasions: silence rather than words for one, or words rather than silence for another; many words in one place on one day, but few in another place on another day. Sensitivity to scripture, to one's surroundings, to intuition, and ultimately to the voice of the Holy Spirit, are all most important; indeed they are much more important than 'getting it right' in any legalistic or formulaic sense.

Sometimes we may find experiences of the holy to be confusing, and we may not know what to do. Perhaps the best-known example of this in scripture is the response of Peter to the transfiguration of Jesus. Finding themselves alone with Jesus, on a high mountain, Peter, James and John see Jesus transfigured by dazzling light, and have a vision of Elijah and Moses standing with Jesus. They are terrified. Not knowing what to say, Peter suggests making tents for Jesus, Moses and Elijah.[11] The encouraging thing about this story is that Peter's confusion does not seem to interrupt events at all. The vision, the voice of God, and the transfiguration of Jesus just continue as though Peter had said nothing. If we are confused by what is happening, we are confused and that will not prevent God from being with us or us from being aware of his presence.

If the first rule is not to treat holy places too lightly, the second rule may therefore be that we shouldn't be too self-conscious, too obsessed with doing the right thing. Such places are what they are because of God's presence, and it is that presence which should be the focus of our attention rather than our own self-consciousness.

If our attention is to be focused on God, however, if we are to 'find' God in a holy place, I think that we do also have to be aware of other things. In particular, I think that we need to be aware of what is going on in some of the inner places that we find inside ourselves: who we are, what we bring with us, our reactions to where we are, ways in which we might pray, and what is distracting. I would like to say a little about each of these in turn.

Who We Are
In the same place, different people will still be different people, and an awareness of our differences can be very helpful in prayer. Among many ways of analysing differences in personality, the Myers-Briggs Type Inventory (MBTI) has proved to be one of the more helpful ways of understanding how differences in personality might be related to differences in spirituality and prayer.[12] It is also helpful in illuminating different responses to place, and especially the holy places that are the subject of this book. The interested reader is encouraged to undertake further reading and to seek the assistance of a registered MBTI consultant in getting a better grasp of how the MBTI works and establishing properly what their own type is.

A place like Durham Cathedral offers so much for different personality types that it is difficult to imagine that anyone will not find something there to appreciate. Extroverts will, of course, enjoy visiting in company, and introverts will appreciate solitude and silence for their visit. The former will want to talk, and the latter will want to read and reflect quietly about the place. For some people the visit will be planned, and for others it will be spontaneous. Whichever approach we take, it may well affect what we find.

When it comes to literal places – such as cathedrals or churches, places of pilgrimage, or other geographical, historical and natural places – the physical senses will obviously be an important part of the process of perceiving what we find. In metaphorical places – our reflections, prayers and meditations – our perceptions will rely more on our memory and imagination. Some of us are likely to find the literal places easier to manage, and others will be more naturally at home in their imagination. For the former it is likely to be colour, sight, sound and smell, history and the beauty of details, that takes the attention, while the latter will be exploring symbolism and meaning, images and the beauty of the whole. However, literal places can be imagined, and metaphorical places can find their symbols in the literal ('real') world, so the former can help in the exploration of the latter, and vice versa, for both types. Both may find an awareness of God's presence, but it is likely to be perceived in different ways – or at least from different starting points.

Similarly, responses to a holy place are likely to vary according to personality type. Some will respond by explaining, questioning, and understanding. Others will respond on the basis of their own or other people's feelings. Both types may find that an engagement with the story behind the place provides the basis for a response in service to others, but for the former it would more likely be concerned with pursuit of justice, and for the latter with the particular needs of individuals or groups.

If holy places are places in which we find God, and if prayer is about finding God, different people will find different kinds of prayer helpful in the search. For some it might be helpful to use written, structured or vocal prayers, for others a more contemplative approach will be more helpful.

The general principle is that different personalities, in the same place, will find that different kinds of prayer come more naturally or are more helpful. So . . . When praying in a holy place do use forms of prayer that you find most helpful for you, and don't force yourself to pray in ways that are completely unproductive. On the other hand, do be prepared to experiment sometimes and to try things that you wouldn't normally find helpful. Be open to things that you might easily have overlooked. 'Distractions' can turn out to be things with unconscious or symbolic significance. Look at details, but also look at the whole of what you see. Be aware of how you feel, as well as what you are thinking. Pay at least some attention to things that seem to be unimportant.

What We Bring

When we come into a holy place, we bring with us not only our personality and preferences, but also our whole life history and circumstances. This includes the things that worry or delight us, the decisions and plans that we need to make or have made, our regrets and shame, our hopes and fears, our deepest desires. It is good that we bring these things with us, for they provide the link between the rest of our lives and our (usually all too brief) time in the holy place. However, they do present us with a choice. Will we use our time in this place to seek God, or to pray about all of these things that concern us?

We can, of course, revisit holy places, and we might well use our time in such places differently on different occasions, or else we might use a single visit both to pray about the concerns that we bring with us and to seek God for his own sake. Ideally, the things that we bring will become things that will draw us to search for God more earnestly, and our search for God will also lead us to the place in which all these other concerns will be put into proportion. However, sometimes they do lead us to confront and identify our own priorities. What do we really want most deeply? If I only have five minutes here, do I most want to use it to find God because of sheer love for him, or do I most want God to meet my immediate needs? In any case, what are my real needs, as I perceive them? And what are they as seen through God's eyes?

However we decide to use a particular time of prayer, it is important to acknowledge the concerns, worries and needs that we bring with us. Even if we determine that on this occasion they are going to be put to one side, we need to be aware of them, if only in order mentally to place them in God's safe keeping for the brief period of time in which we have come to focus on other things.

Our Reactions To Where We Are

An awareness of our surroundings can be helpful. What comes first to your attention when you enter this place? Where do you feel you are most drawn to – and why? What do you see, hear, feel, or even taste or smell? What do these things say about this place – or about God – or about you? Becoming too preoccupied with these things is unlikely to be helpful, but allowing a brief pause to reflect upon them can be rewarding. Perhaps standing inside a doorway, or sitting briefly at the edge of a place, can allow a choice to be made about where it would be most helpful to sit, or kneel, or stand for this time of prayer. More intuitive types might use this time simply to become aware of where that place is, and others might more consciously identify the details of what attracts them to a particular area within a holy place, but either way the time can be well spent and can help in finding a place in which you 'belong' and can most easily or productively pray on this occasion. Having moved to that chosen place, it can similarly be helpful to spend a few moments reflecting on whether it might be best to sit, or stand, or kneel, or even lie down. And then again, having adopted this posture, there will be a time of becoming aware of what it is like simply to be there. What can be seen, heard, felt or sensed in other ways in this place?

Ways of Praying

There are many ways of praying. If there are repeated opportunities to pray in a particularly holy place, then it may well be helpful to experiment, and to move beyond the familiar. Liturgical prayer, contemplative prayer, prayer with a rosary or other repetitive prayers (such as the Jesus prayer), extemporary prayer, imaginative prayer and others all have their place.

Praying with words, or simply being silent can both be helpful, and sometimes one might seem more appropriate than another, or there might be a natural rhythm of moving from one to another. Praying about, or with, what we see or hear can similarly be helpful at different times or to a different degree. Perhaps an icon, or a stained glass window, or a feature of the natural landscape, might catch our attention and become a point of focus that expresses our prayers, our feelings, or our desire for God. Some of us need to be wary of rushing too hastily from such awareness into a multitude of words, but equally there can come a point when the silence of contemplating such things can most helpfully be transformed into words. Or perhaps our contemplation is better expressed in the lighting of a candle, or a move from kneeling to sitting (or vice versa), or making the sign of the cross, or in some other way.

At other times, attention jumps too rapidly from one object to another in the environment, or from one thought to another in the mind, and there is no sense of focus. Or perhaps there is too much focus on something – a curiosity about something unimportant, or about something very important. Any sense of the numinous is excluded by attention to these thoughts and perceptions. Sometimes, these 'distractions' can actually prove to be important (see below) – but often they are more an impediment to prayer. In these cases, it is good to express in words the sense of frustration that we feel and to try to focus on a particular object or prayer. The Jesus Prayer can be very helpful here. Simply to repeat: 'Jesus Christ, Son of God, have mercy on me a sinner', over and over, can help to bring focus and stillness to a busy and distracted mind.

Another way of bringing focus is to find a passage of scripture and to use this as a basis for our prayers. This might be a passage that finds resonance in some way with our present life circumstances or with the place in which we are praying. It might be a passage that lends itself to a more imaginative style of meditation, in which we imagine ourselves as present in, or observing, the narrative. With whom do we identify? What do we see, hear, touch, taste or smell? How do we feel about being in this place in our imagination? What happens? If the passage is from the gospels, it can often be especially helpful to explore any interaction that we might have with Jesus himself. Such imaginative prayer can take time, and it is good to record our experiences in a journal and to discuss them later with an experienced retreat director or spiritual director.

With practice, it is possible to be still and to empty the mind of all thoughts and distractions, or at least simply to acknowledge them as they arise and then to put them to one side as they come into mind. Just to 'be' in the presence of God, to be aware of his presence in silence, can be a very powerful form of prayer. Sometimes, it is this that seems to express all that really matters, and our fussy insistence on praying specifically about particular things can seem to be the biggest distraction of all from true prayer. All things find their unity in God. He knows our needs, and he knows better than we do how to meet them. What else of any value can we desire other than God himself?

What Distracts Us

When praying in a holy place, or in any place, we need, then, to be reverently focused on God, not too self-conscious, not too intense, but simply open to what God may – or may not – give us in our prayers. But herein lies one of the biggest challenges of prayer, for any attempt at a reverent and open focus on God encounters the all too human phenomenon of distraction. Distractions seem to assume an even greater variety of forms than do encounters with God, or at least every potential encounter with God would seem to be vulnerable to an infinite multitude of possible encounters with things that are other than God. Things we forgot to do, something that we did that we regret, things that we need to do, things that are going on just a short distance away, the heat, the cold, the hardness of the seat or floor, the light, the dark, the pictures on the wall, the person who has just walked in, something we thought we heard, the time, the inscription that we can't quite read high up on the church wall, something we read once and can't quite remember, and so very many other things all clamour for our attention. In the process, it seems as though we are prevented by a thousand voices from hearing the voice of God. A myriad of things before our eyes prevent us from seeing God. The many distract us from the one, trivialities distract us from that which alone is needful.

A part of the problem here is simply the busyness of our lives. Prayer needs time, and it takes time to put all the affairs of our lives to one side in order that we can pray. The reality is that we bring ourselves, our lives, our concerns, our memories, our plans, and everything that we are concerned about into every place of prayer. It cannot be any other way, and should not be any other way. Our prayers must engage with the reality of our lives, or rather they should be a place of God's engagement with our lives, or else we are just hiding ourselves away and avoiding life.

For all the problems that they present, 'distractions' not infrequently turn out to be ways in which we become aware of the presence of God with us in our prayers. In other words, they prove not to be distractions at all, but rather they are ways in which God is meeting with us. For example, I have found myself fascinated by the many vacant niches in the Neville Screen in Durham Cathedral; by the numbers of statues of saints that they must once have accommodated, and by wondering what happened to those statues when they were removed at the time of the Reformation. At times, this has been 'distracting'. But I have also been led by these thoughts to contemplate the great communion of saints of which I am a part. These distracting features of the stonework have become reminders of the many saints who have followed Christ before me, and whose example encourages me in my own desire to follow him as they did. In this sense, they are not distractions at all. They are – at least for me – a part of what makes that particular part of Durham Cathedral a 'holy' place.

This propensity of material things, and the affairs of this world, to be both distraction from God and revealing of God seems to me to be a manifestation of the paradox with which we started this chapter. God is present everywhere, and yet we find him at particular places at particular times. We must somehow make ourselves receptive to God in such a way that we are not distracted by that which is other than God, but also in such a way that we do not fail to see God in the apparently insignificant. Everything around us is pervaded by God, but everything is potentially distracting from God. Attempts to find God, even in holy places, can be bewildering and confusing, or else profoundly simple. God can be obscured by everything, and hidden by nothing.

I do not think that there is a simple formula that cuts through this problem, but it seems to me to be summed up in the story of Mary

and Martha. For many people, perhaps especially for women who have
adopted a traditional role in the home, this story is a hard one. Mary
and Martha are two sisters, entertaining Jesus in their home. Martha is
busy with all the practicalities of making Jesus welcome, but these tasks
keep her away from Jesus. Mary is neglectful of the practical realities of
hospitality, but is devoted to Jesus' every word. When Jesus commends
Mary for this, it feels to us to be unfair on Martha. But Jesus does not
say that the chores do not need to be done, and his words to Martha
are not unsympathetic; his concern for her distress is evident:

> Martha, Martha, you are worried and distracted by many things;
> there is need of only one thing.[13]

Jesus clearly does not want Martha to be worried or distracted, and she
is equally clearly distressed by her distractions. A single-hearted focus
on Jesus seems to be what she and Jesus both implicitly recognize as
necessary and desirable. That this is not what Martha finds here must
be a result of many factors, but it is definitely not what either she or
Jesus really want. It is Mary's focus on the one thing that is needful
that is commended, and that is what Martha is encouraged to emulate.

Martha is that part of every woman, and of every man, which is
sad and frustrated at the way in which things seem to get in the way
of finding God. Mary is that part of every woman, and every man,
which desires to find God. Somehow, in the ordering of the affairs of
our hearts and lives we have to find a way of focusing on the one thing
that is needful. Mary must be given space to be Mary, for there will be
plenty of time for the Martha within each of us to attend to her affairs.

Finding God in a Holy Place

If I am right in asserting that prayer is all about finding God, then
prayer is full of paradoxes. How can anyone ever have faith in God who
does not first have at least enough faith to embark on the search for
God that is prayer? It seems that we need faith to pray, but we need first
to pray, if we are to have faith. And how can we go about searching for
something, or rather *someone*, who is everywhere – even deep within
ourselves? If we don't find him in the present moment and place, even
though we know that he *is* here, then why go anywhere else to look for
him? Moreover, I have suggested that although a search for God is a
search for that which is wholly *other* than ourselves, it also involves us
in looking deeply *within* ourselves.

Similarly, the whole idea of holy places seems to be self-contradictory. At least, it is contradictory to suggest that any one place might be more holy than any other if it is also true that the holy God is equally present in all places and in every place. But, our daily experience suggests to us that we don't in fact live in a monochrome, undifferentiated, universe within which all places are completely holy and good. Just as a completely white picture on a completely white background would appear invisible to us, the very possibility of finding God requires us at least to be able to imagine that God is not present in some places and in some times, so that we can see him in the times and places where he is present in contrast with those where he is not. In fact, we don't have to imagine this at all – it is exactly the way that things appear to us to be in day-to-day reality – but it is only when we have begun to see him in this way in some places that we might be able to begin to see him in other places where we thought that he was absent.

To change the metaphor slightly, searching for God in prayer is perhaps like looking for a particular kind of shell, a shell that we have never seen before, on a beach that is full of shells. At first we find it difficult even to imagine what we are looking for. And then a friend shows us one of these shells and suddenly we *know* what we are looking for. Quickly we find another, and then another. Eventually, we realize that the whole beach is covered with these shells – in different shapes and sizes, in different colours, some broken and some complete. The problem was not that the shells weren't there. The problem was within us – our own inability to imagine what this kind of shell is like, and what is distinctive about it, and then even to begin to know where to look for it amidst so much diversity and such a great expanse of beach.

Holy places are like these shells. They come in many different shapes and sizes and colours, but they are all recognisably the same. Once we have found one then it becomes easier to find others, and the more we have found the more we want to find. Paradoxically, we have to want to search before we have seen just how beautiful they are, but perhaps (to extend the metaphor slightly) our first encounter will come quite unexpectedly, at a point in our lives when we were not searching at all. It is as though someone else held up a shell as we were passing, and we caught a glimpse of how beautiful it was. Then we find ourselves engaged in our own search. But once we have caught a glimpse of the beauty, mystery and wonder of one shell, of one holy place, then we are spurred on to find others.

This book is written for fellow searchers who have not known where to begin, or who have been discouraged, or who have got lost in their search. In a sense, I am holding up a single, very beautiful, shell in the midst of a beach that is full of shells that vary in colour, size and completeness. I offer it only as an example of what can be found. It is to encourage others to begin their own search in other parts of the beach. What they find will undoubtedly look different in all kinds of ways, but it will also be very recognisably, and very certainly, the same.

I am not suggesting that it is not possible to think that we have found what we are looking for and be mistaken. Sometimes, through lack of imagination, through lack of vision or experience or knowledge, or through a feeling of failure in the search, or else just because we are looking in the wrong place, we might think we have found (or wish to think we have found) what we are looking for when, in fact, we have not. However, if we are not to be deceived I think that we do need to pay attention to what fellow searchers (the Christian saints who have gone before us) have found. Only in this way can we begin to distinguish what it is that we are really looking for.

❦

Exploring Inner Places

This chapter concludes with some suggested ways in which to reflect on visiting holy places within ourselves. They might be used as a way of reviewing where you have got to in your past explorations of prayer and as a way of preparing to explore new places of prayer in the future.

What 'places' have you already visited in prayer, recently and during the longer course of your life? In reflecting on the answer to this question, think firstly about the metaphorical places in which you began to pray and to which you have been: places of need, places of faith (or lack of it), places of sorrow and joy, places of relationship with others and of being alone, places of imagination and of painful reality, places in time. Do you pray about problems, or do you have problems with prayer? Where have you found it easiest to pray? Where have you found it most difficult to pray? Where have you found God, and where has God seemed to be absent? What approaches to prayer (liturgy, sacraments, extempore prayer, meditation on scripture, etc.) have you found most helpful in each of these places? Who has helped you to find your way from place to place? (Include here books and writings as well as people you have known.) In which place did your journey start?

Think also about the literal, geographical, places in which you have prayed. Which places, and which kinds of places, have most helped you in your prayers? Are your surroundings a distraction, or do they help your prayers? (Do you pray with your eyes closed or open? Why?) Do you find candles, icons or incense helpful? Where do you find it most difficult to pray?

In the light of these reflections, what expectations, hopes and fears do you bring with you to the holy place(s) in which you will seek to engage with the explorations of prayer outlined in this book – whether this be Durham Cathedral or elsewhere?

You may like to conclude with a prayer such as the one that follows, which is by St Ignatius of Loyola (c.1491–1556). Ignatius devised a challenging set of spiritual exercises, which combine the search for God in the inner world with a search for personal vocation. He concludes, and expects us to conclude, that we should offer back to God in love and service all that we have – including our memories, expectations, hopes and fears, as well as material things. If you don't feel able to offer yourself this completely to God, then don't pray this prayer! However, Ignatius challenges us to find our own happiness in love and service of God:

Take, Lord, and receive all my liberty, my memory, my understanding, and my entire will, all that I have and possess. You gave it all to me; to you Lord I give it all back. All is yours, dispose of it entirely according to your will. Give me the grace to love you, for that is enough for me.[14]

Durham Cathedral from Observatory Hill

Chapter 3

An Invitation to Pray: The Nave and the Body of the Church

The nave of Durham Cathedral creates a dramatic first impression. The huge columns on either side of the central aisle induce a timeless sense of solidity and majesty. Their enormous height draws the gaze upwards to heaven. Their girth makes the columns of other cathedrals seem spindly and fragile by comparison. And their procession eastwards, along the nave and then flanking the quire, draws the eyes towards the huge rose window situated high up in the east wall of the Cathedral. In this window, the 12 apostles and 24 elders of the book of Revelation[1] are portrayed surrounding Christ the King who, in its centre, is shown reigning over all things in eternal majesty. It is an awe-inspiring sight, and I never cease to appreciate it, even though I have now made hundreds of visits to the Cathedral over several years of living in Durham.

If the nave evokes awe, it also evokes other feelings. A 9-year-old boy, when confronted with a view of the nave from the west crossing, and being asked by his guide how the Cathedral made him feel, said that it 'sort of wraps its arms round you'![2] Such a large space cannot easily be called intimate, yet it is certainly enveloping and welcoming, as though drawing the visitor in. But what does it draw people into?

Although divine services were the main purpose for which the nave was constructed, it was only used once each week for this purpose in monastic times. The Jesus Mass was held each Friday at the Jesus altar, in front of the screen that was then between the last two pillars at the eastern end. Few people seem to spend longer than a few minutes here today, unless they have come for a service. This may be partly because there is always something going on: even in the early morning, the nave is rarely quiet for long. Tourists are almost always to be found here; clergy, vergers, choristers, stewards, workmen, cleaners, flower arrangers, guides and others go about their business; but I don't think that it is only this that makes it difficult to stop and reflect.

There is so much else to do, there are so many other parts of the Cathedral to visit, that it always feels tempting (especially on a first visit) to move on from the nave. Just as the huge Norman columns draw the gaze towards the east rose window, so they tend to draw the visitor to walk in that direction. Or perhaps it is just a reflection of the busyness of all our lives that we all tend to move on too quickly all the time, which makes contemplative or meditative prayer difficult at any time or in any place.

But I have also found that this place has helped me to pray. It has helped me to explore things that are difficult to put into words. It has helped me to find stillness amidst all the busyness and distractions that life presents. It has helped me to be aware of the presence of God and to listen to God. If we take the time to stop and listen, this place actually invites us to pray.

The tiered Norman arches of the Nave

Construction

The nave of Durham Cathedral is a humanly constructed space for prayer. It has come to be the place that it currently is as a result of the creative plans of human beings. It was built in just 40 years, from 1093 to 1133. It represented significant technical advances in its time, with the first use of buttresses to enable greater height, and ribbed vaulting and pointed arches to enable the use of stone vaulting. The result was a higher stone ceiling over the central aisle than had previously been considered possible. This contributes to the impact created by the huge scale: 61 metres in length, 12 metres wide, and 22 metres high.

The nave comprises a series of double and single bays, separated by compound columns that extend the full height of the Cathedral. The bays accommodate three tiers of Norman arches. The round columns that divide each double bay into two are proportioned such that their height is equal to their circumference. Quite apart from the symbolic significance of this geometry,[3] this further contributes to the sense of height, solidity and scale of the nave.

In addition to the tiers of arches, the architecture has tiers of historical associations. The architectural style is actually Romanesque, echoing the forms of classical Roman architecture. In the Middle Ages the interior decoration also included wall painting, which has now all but completely vanished, but the simplicity of the natural sandstone that remains today is still both elegant and beautiful.

The construction of the nave provides an overarching sense of space. There is timelessness and a sense of eternity within the nave, an aura of permanence and stability. It speaks of something unchanging that transcends time and space; it has an almost numinous quality, providing a context within which an encounter with the divine somehow feels more likely or more possible.

The nave also affords a variety of places within which to sit or kneel for quiet reflection or prayer. The perspective offered is different depending upon where one chooses to sit or stand. The best perspective upon the overall architecture and the best overall sense of elevation and scale is provided by sitting near to the central aisle, and towards the west end of the nave. On the other hand, a series of more intimate and less visible places to sit may be found near to the north and south walls, between the huge columns that support the roof. Eight of these spaces are adjacent to a stained glass window, each of which offers its own particular focus for meditation and prayer. And then, again, nearer to the front of the nave, the transepts, tower and quire come more into view, each with their own perspectives of height, breadth and depth.

The construction of places for a particular purpose, and in a particular way, does not in itself make them holy. Doubtless many places constructed for holiness (some churches included) completely fail to achieve it in any readily observable way. Other places, not made to be holy, achieve or acquire a holiness all of their own, through human experience, or perhaps through a life-changing encounter with God. Holiness may be very specific – experienced by some people and not others – or it may be tangible to many. The kind of holiness of place that is appreciated by almost everyone, or at least by most people, is much more difficult to define. Perhaps some of this holiness has to do with what almost everyone knows about the place, as when a Hindu colleague of mine commented (when I was working in Canterbury) that he had been to Canterbury Cathedral and could tell that it was a place in which many prayers had been offered over the years. Or perhaps the holiness that he sensed arose because he knew that this was a place of prayer, rather than the other way around. The place of Thomas Becket's martyrdom is a particularly holy place within Canterbury Cathedral, but it feels even holier when you have stood there and heard the eyewitness accounts of what happened there. Sometimes knowing the story of the place is an important part of holiness.

By contrast, some places seem to be holy by virtue of human construction or the work of nature. It is as though the form and fabric of these places traces the shape of letters that spell out words of holiness legible to the human mind at some subliminal level of consciousness. I don't think that these letters or words have to be written on a large scale. The frequency with which people refer to mountain-top experiences, or are moved by a starlit sky, or find the sheer size of cathedral buildings breathtaking, does seem to suggest that scale is at least one word in the vocabulary of this language of holy places, but sometimes the scale of holiness can be very small, rather than very large, as in the experience of Julian of Norwich:

> And [our Lord] showed me more, a little thing, the size of a hazelnut, on the palm of my hand, round like a ball. I looked at it thoughtfully and wondered, 'What is this?' And the answer came, 'It is all that is made.' I marvelled that it continued to exist and did not suddenly disintegrate; it was so small. And again my mind supplied the answer, 'It exists, both now and for ever, because God loves it.'[4]

If scale is one of the words in this vocabulary, there are clearly others to be learned, and amongst them I think that colour and light must feature prominently.

Colour and Light

The nave of Durham Cathedral incorporates both dark and light in proportions which vary with the weather and the seasons. I most enjoy the effect in the early morning, in summer, before the artificial lighting is turned on. It then becomes clear that the interior of the Cathedral is actually a darkness penetrated by light from outside and within – especially from windows and candles. The high clerestory windows illuminate and draw attention to the ceiling vaults and this draws the eye upwards. Shafts of summer sunlight penetrate corners of the darkness of the Cathedral, creating beautiful and varying effects. But there is also still enough darkness left for the candles to dispel in their own, very different, fashion.

Much of the light from outside is transmitted through clear glass. Emanating from a rising or setting sun, or from the brightness of midday, it throws a wash of varying shades of red, yellow, cream or white (and in winter grey) upon the varying taupes, yellows and reds of the sandstone within. Other shafts of light, being transmitted through stained glass, are split into abstract multicoloured patterns on the same sandstone background. At yet other times, when there is only darkness outside, candles and electric lights produce another kind of mystery – of illumination in the midst of darkness. Different kinds of light at different times of day and night thus produce many and varied shades and colours, contrasting with each other and with the shadows that always linger beneath the Norman arches and behind the huge columns. It is a beauty which is not adequately conveyed by words, or even photographs, and which seems somehow infused with the mystery of a created order both beyond and yet also deeply within this world.

The beauty of this overall effect of refracted and reflected light, originating both from within and from without, is complemented by the more vivid and detailed stories told by the stained glass. The colour in the glass, arising from refraction of light that enters the Cathedral from without, draws the eye and invites reflection within upon the various stories that it tells.

The visitor standing at the west end of the nave finds her eye drawn first by the procession of columns towards the large rose window in the east end of the Cathedral, visible above the screen that separates the nave and crossing from the quire. At the centre of this window is Christ in glory. At the opposite end of the nave is a large window depicting a 'Jesse tree' – showing the human descent and lineage of Christ, including scenes of the visitation of the Virgin Mary by an angel to announce her part in this plan (the 'annunciation') and the visitation of the infant Christ by the Magi. At the pinnacle of this huge window are symbols of God as Father, Son and Holy Spirit.[5]

The theme of the northern saints, and of the bringing of Christianity to the northeast of England, is represented by a series of windows in the wall of the south aisle, and a number of other colourful windows are visible from the nave. But the windows that most attract attention in the nave are the Jesse tree in the west and the rose window in the east. Of these, it is the latter that provides the true visual focus, as the Cathedral is oriented in this direction, and the former is therefore usually only seen when leaving the Cathedral via the exits at the western end. The huge central aisle of the nave thus takes the visitor on a journey from west to east, from one huge stained glass window to another. But the nave also offers spaces between and behind its enormous pillars, where different and more intimate places are formed.

The lighting and colour and symbolism provided by the windows characterize and differentiate the spaces within the nave in which one may pause to reflect or pray. In addition to the windows, light comes from candles within the bays at the east end of the nave. These are provided for visitors to light as a visible token or sign of their prayers. The lighting of candles in prayer is an ancient tradition, and one that many people engage in instinctively rather than with any definite awareness of exactly why they do it. But it also acknowledges at some more or less unconscious level that prayer is about a human desire to bring divine light into dark places in this world.

In the bay near to the southwest door (leading into the cloister) there is the dark seventeenth-century Spanish woodwork of the miners' memorial on the south wall. The words inscribed on the memorial remind the visitor of the physical 'darkness and danger' encountered by those who have worked in the coal mines which have been such a major feature of the life of northeast England since the industrial revolution. Although these mines have now closed locally, the landscape and community of the northeast is still shaped by the legacy that they left. This detail of the nave symbolizes a dark exterior landscape of northeast England, a place that in its worst abuses of economic power at the cost of human life has been almost the opposite of 'holy' and yet which is also loved by many and has been made holy by the lives of saints and of ordinary people who have given their lives to it. The unemployment and poverty of this post-industrial landscape today are a kind of darkness. And yet, the annual miners' gala continues to bring large numbers of local people into the Cathedral each year, and is not a sombre affair. It is full of life, colour and celebration.

Darkness, light, and colour, then, appear to be three more words in our vocabulary of holy places. Themes of light penetrating darkness, reminiscent of the prologue of John's gospel, are a prominent feature of the environment that the nave provides:

> The light shines in the darkness, and the darkness did not overcome it.[6]

This invites us to pray that the light of Christ will shine also in the darkness of our own lives, and that it will not be overcome. Sometimes prayers at such difficult times are more helpfully undertaken in silence, making more use of symbols of light and darkness than of many words. We might find such symbols in churches, like Durham Cathedral. But they are also to be found in the sky at dawn or sunset, in the light of a candle in our own homes, in the reflections of sunlight playing on water, by a fireside, in a painting or photograph, and in many other places. Such places can help to give expression to our prayers, and to remind us that the light of Christ shines in the deepest darkness, and that it has not been overcome.

Space and Time

One of the most powerful effects created by the nave is a sense of timelessness. Of humanly built structures that I have seen, I can only compare this with the great pyramids in Egypt. It seems to me that this sense of timelessness is partly due to the sheer scale of the structure, and is partly evoked by the Romanesque architecture, but it also remains partly elusive of explanation. Despite the distractions, it is possible to sit down here and feel somehow removed from the world outside, as though suspended in time.

Doubtless this depends to some extent upon one's purpose for being in the Cathedral, and one's attitude to being there. The hurried tourists on their demanding holiday itinerary and the graduating students attending carefully timetabled congregations hardly appear to be in a world in which time has been suspended. But the solitary figure who lights a candle and sits or kneels in prayer, even if only for a few minutes, seems to have entered a different place altogether. It is this place which I experience when I pray here, and not only when I pray in the formal sense but when I am just *here* with enough recollection of mind to be aware of it. It is this place that is timeless.

This timelessness is, it seems to me, located within an axis of time that is defined both sacramentally and by the stained glass. On the one hand, the nave is located between sacramental points of reference of the font, situated at the west end, and the altar, situated at the east end.[7] On the other hand, the nave is located between two stained glass windows – the Jesse tree in the west, and Christ in glory in the east. It therefore lies on a kind of time line, on the one hand between baptism and Eucharist, and on the other hand between the earthly incarnation of Christ in human form and a vision of the divine Christ in heavenly glory.

The font, as the place of baptism, is traditionally located (here as in other churches) near to the main door, and thus at the west end. The altar, by contrast, is located at the east end, so that the congregation faces east. Baptism marks the beginning of Christian life, being a sign of entry into, and belonging to, the Church as the body of Christ. The Eucharist, on the other hand, is a participation in Christ's passion, a sacrament reserved for those who are Christ's followers, who are called to take up their cross and lay down their lives for Christ. Because the central aisle of the nave is located on a symbolic axis between the places in which these sacraments are celebrated, it represents the Christian pilgrimage from sharing in his baptism to sharing in his passion. This is the journey of following Christ in life in this world – from the point of finding faith in Christ until the time of dying in faith, in hope of eternal life with him.

All of this is expressed in the words of one of the verses of the prayer known as 'St Patrick's breastplate'. Different verses of this prayer will appear at different points through this book as expressing, in an early Irish form, some of the themes that this holy place invites us to reflect upon. The first full verse of the prayer invites us to identify with, or participate in, or 'bind' to ourselves, Christ's baptism, death and resurrection:

> I bind this today to me forever
> By power of faith, Christ's incarnation;
> His baptism in Jordan river,
> His death on Cross for my salvation;
> His bursting from the spicèd tomb,
> His riding up the heavenly way,

> His coming at the day of doom
> I bind unto myself today.[8]

The stained glass windows also define a timeline, but this is in reference to the longer perspective of Christ as the eternal Son of God, rather than to Christian followers in their journey from sharing in Christ's baptism to sharing in his death. This timeline extends back to the origin of all things in Christ, and it looks forward to the end of all things in Christ.

Looking back in time, the west window provides a reference in history to the human lineage of Christ, and especially to his birth of Mary. Prior to the incarnation of Christ, human life was lived as a part of the story that the west window tells. While the window is very specific, in that it tells the story of the birth of Jesus in relation to the Hebrew people from whom he found human descent, it is more broadly representative of the birth of the Christ in relation to the whole human family, with which he identified and of which he became a part.

But the Trinitarian symbols in the apex of the west window remind us that even this is not the real beginning of the Christian story. The incarnation of Christ as a human being within time proceeds from the eternal begetting of Christ as Son from the Father, as God from God. In the prologue to John's gospel, this is expressed in terms of the eternal divine principle – the 'Word' of God – becoming human flesh. In this way the eternal is expressed in human form; that which is timeless is expressed within time. In the words of John's gospel:

> And the Word became flesh and lived among us, and we have seen his glory, the glory as of a father's only son, full of grace and truth.[9]

Similarly, looking forward in time, the east window provides a reference to the eternal glory of Christ in heaven, in hope of which all Christians are called to live. This window, based upon the vision of St John as recorded in the book of Revelation, finds Christ reigning over all things, and receiving eternal praise in words that are repeated in the Cathedral at every celebration of the Eucharist:

> Holy, holy, holy,
> the Lord God the Almighty,
> who was and is and is to come[10]

Similarly, the 24 elders portrayed in the window are recorded by John as eternally offering praise to Christ:

> You are worthy, our Lord and God,
> to receive glory and honour and power,
> for you created all things,
> and by your will they existed and were created.[11]

Thus, the east and west windows define a timeline which extends beyond the limits of time, into eternity. Both the beginning and the end of this line are to be found in Christ and all human life is lived in relation to it. The origin and destiny of all human beings, and of all things – even time itself – is found in Christ.

Life within time, within the Cathedral and in every place, is situated in the midst of eternity, between the coming of Christ into the world from eternity, and the fulfilment and end of all things in Christ in eternity. But here, in this sacred space within the Cathedral, we are also reminded that Christ is with us in the present. We are reminded of this perhaps especially at sacramental occasions of baptism and Eucharist. But Christ is also with us here when we come to him in prayer alone, or with others, or when we are alone here with others in our hearts. So, the Cathedral reminds us that Christ is both behind us and before us, beside us and within us, within us and within others. Again, this is expressed well by one of the verses of St Patrick's prayer:

> Christ be with me, Christ within me,
> Christ behind me, Christ before me,
> Christ beside me, Christ to win me,
> Christ to comfort and restore me.
> Christ beneath me, Christ above me,
> Christ in quiet, Christ in danger,
> Christ in hearts of all that love me,
> Christ in mouth of friend and stranger.[12]

Although it is most unlikely that the majority of visitors to Durham Cathedral consciously reflect upon or recognize the symbolism that I have described here, nonetheless, the east and west windows and the font and the altar are highly visible features at each end of the nave. Such features are common to most churches. To those who stop to reflect upon their significance, they locate the present life of the Christian within the boundaries of time that they represent. Perhaps even to

48 *Finding God in a Holy Place*

those who do not consciously stop and reflect on this, they have some unconscious impact.

To the extent that in reality most human lives do not fully orientate themselves according to these reference points, a cathedral or church might be seen as a kind of compass that reminds us of the direction in which we are called to travel as followers of Christ. It offers a reminder that we follow him from new birth in baptism to participation in his suffering and death, and from there to share in his resurrection life in eternal glory.

Durham Cathedral, then, has a timelessness about it, but also anchors our prayers in the context of time. It takes us outside of time, but gives us reference points within time. Other places can be like this and, again, they are not always conventionally holy places. Mountain-top experiences (I mean, literally, being on a mountain top, rather than a metaphorical 'peak experience') convey this by giving us a perspective of a world laid out before us, a world which goes about its business as we watch it, as it were, from outside time. A night sky can do the same kind of thing, except that here we see ourselves within a vast eternity, rather than observing things as though from outside. Another example might be when we find ourselves 'lost' in the reading of a good book. Suddenly, as we put it down, we realize that we are back in the 'real' world. Time has not stopped, after all. But now we see things differently. Our identification with the characters or themes that have temporarily captivated us now helps us to see reality differently. They give us new points of reference for understanding our lives differently.

The Body of Christ

The nave of a cathedral or church is central to congregational worship. At a Sunday Eucharist, the gospel is read and the intercessions are led from the centre of the nave – in symbolism of the proclamation of the gospel and the offering of prayers from within the body of the Church. Sitting alone in the nave early in the morning, the rows of empty seats provide a powerful reminder that this is a place for the body of Christ – that is the community of all those who are baptized into Christ.

This community of believers transcends the present. The stained glass windows portray local saints who have been members of that same body over centuries past: Oswald, Gilpin, Coifi, Paulinus, Aidan, Cuthbert, Benedict Biscop, and Bede. The body of Christ is thus not simply those who meet in this place today for worship and prayer, but those of all times and places who are, and have been, and will be a part of the community that is defined by participation in Christ through faith, baptism and Eucharist. The use of this space for baptism and Eucharist thus redefines, spiritually and sacramentally, what the nave is all about.

In services of baptism, around the font located at the west end of the nave, human beings, God and the wider Church are all brought together in sacramental time and space in such a way that is neither mere symbolism, nor magical action, but more a prayer made visible – a prayer that incorporates new members of the family of Christ into the body of Christ. According to the prologue to John's gospel, the coming of Christ into the world as light into darkness, as Word become flesh, took place in order to make possible this mystical incorporation:

> But to all who received him, who believed in his name, he gave power to become children of God, who were born, not of blood or of the will of the flesh or of the will of man, but of God.[13]

In the Eucharist, represented at the east end of the nave by the altar, members of the family of Christ, God and the Church are again brought together in sacramental time and space. Again, this is neither mere symbolism nor magic, but rather a faithful participation in the body of Christ that is both the assembled congregation and the consecrated bread. In the words of John's gospel, the coming of Christ into the world is understood as having taken place in order that this participation might come about:

> Jesus said to them . . . the bread of God is that which comes down from heaven and gives life to the world . . . I am the bread of life . . .. Those who eat my flesh and drink my blood abide in me, and I in them.[14]

But this body is more than the physical symbolism of font and altar, and it is more even than the sacramental mysteries of baptism and Eucharist. It is a very practical affair. In Matthew's gospel, Jesus tells his listeners that when they feed the hungry, give drink to the thirsty, welcome the stranger, clothe the naked, care for the sick, or visit those in prison, they do it to him.[15] Conversely, if they fail to do these things for others, they fail to do them for him. Prayer in a cathedral or church is not intended to be a hiding away from the world, but rather an equipping for going out into the world.

This going out into the world to be the body of Christ in attending to the bodily needs of others takes place at the end of every baptism and

Eucharist – or at least it does if and when the people who are Christ's body respond positively to this invitation to mission. Of course, the forms that this mission takes can be extremely varied: from participating in the work of charities, to studying and implementing social policy; from working as a nurse or social worker, to giving financially to good causes; from the work of an evangelist to a vocation to prayer. The variety of forms of participation in this mission of the body of Christ is as diverse as the variety of people to whom it is addressed.

People confer holiness on places – by their presence and by their actions.

Place of Invitation

The window to the west of the main north entrance to the Cathedral is an abstract and colourful representation of The Last Supper. As though from above, the 12 disciples are represented as sitting around the table, with Jesus at its head. Each has a piece of bread on the table in front

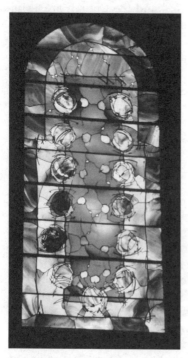

The Daily Bread window

of them. The whole is surrounded by a purple border – a reminder that all things are incorporated within God. But, within this divine reality that encompasses all things, Christ is portrayed as God made flesh, a God who invites men and women to come to his table and share in his body.

There is no chalice on the table, but the table itself is blood red. The cross through the head of Christ and the starry night around the other end of the table are reminders that life can be dark – albeit pierced by light – and painful, and is marred by death, though it is a place of sharing human love, sustenance and friendship. All but one of the figures around this chalice-table are also participants in it, in the sense that they are partly within its boundaries and partly in the world outside it. But one figure, a dark and stormy looking shape, barely touches the boundary of the table. Coming close, touching the perimeter but not entering the space within, it remains outside, a non-participant.

Situated next to the main entrance to the Cathedral, although representing something that usually takes place at the opposite end of the nave, this window seems to me to offer an invitation. It is an invitation that will not be heard by everyone, that will be ignored or rejected by many, and that will be accepted only by some. Will we participate in Christ, in prayer, sacrament and mission; or will we refuse to enter within the boundaries of his Kingdom?

The nearby welcome desk invites visitors to explore the building. But however warm the welcome of the volunteers who staff it, most visitors will not go on to become a part of the community that the building represents. The font nearby similarly invites the person who comes into this building, if they will stop and reflect upon the invitation, to become a participant in the body of Christ. But many will not accept this invitation either. Among those who count themselves as Christ's disciples, there is also an invitation to share in communion – to participate in his body and blood. All[16] of those who call themselves Christians will accept this invitation at one level, but at another level it represents an invitation that is far more challenging, and there are diverse reasons for not accepting it.

Apart from simple non-belief there is, for example, a perceived sense of unworthiness such as that expressed eloquently in the first line of George Herbert's famous poem:

> Love bade me welcome: yet my soul drew back,
> Guilty of dust and sin.[17]

For Herbert, awareness of unworthiness, shame, and ingratitude were a reason for immediately declining the invitation of Christ (whom he represents as Love). As Love overcomes Herbert's objections, one by one, he is eventually compelled to 'sit and eat' at the table prepared for him.

But another response is to accept the invitation too willingly, too quickly to suggest that it has been considered properly. When Mark gives an account of the request of James and John, that they might sit either side of Jesus when he is seated in glory, he reports that Jesus told the two disciples that they did not know what they were asking. Jesus then questions them:

'Are you able to drink the cup that I drink, or be baptised with the baptism that I am baptised with?' They replied 'We are able.' Then Jesus said to them, 'The cup that I drink you will drink; and with the baptism with which I am baptised, you will be baptised; but to sit at my right hand or my left is not mine to grant, but it is for those for whom it has been prepared.'[18]

Taking the chalice – the cup – that Christ was offered, participating in his passion and death as well as in his life and love, is far more challenging than most realize when they first accept the invitation to be his followers. But the invitation is offered at different levels and in different ways, not only in the nave of Durham Cathedral, or in other churches, but most especially in the wider world outside. The nave of a church provides just one space within which the depth and challenge of this invitation may be explored. It invites us to come in, to be part of something greater, higher, more solid and more mysterious than ourselves. It invites us into a timeless space within our lives within which we can explore the implications of the invitation that Christ offers to us all. To respond too quickly to this invitation suggests that we have not considered it carefully enough.

Invitation, Story and Personality

Our responses to invitations to pray will be influenced by our personality. Perhaps this is best illustrated by the story of Mary and Martha just before the resurrection of Lazarus (which may be found in Chapter 11 of John's gospel). Jesus has delayed coming to Bethany until Lazarus (the brother of Mary and Martha) has died. When he finally arrives he is greeted first by Martha, and then by Mary. Each sister, independently of the other, greets Jesus with exactly the same words: 'Lord, if you had been here, my brother would not have died'[19]. But Martha then engages with Jesus in conversation about faith and resurrection whereas Mary simply cries. Jesus is ready to talk with Martha and cry with Mary, but the prayers of both sisters are answered when Lazarus comes out of the tomb in response to Jesus' command.

Just as Mary and Martha responded differently to the similar emotional place in which they found themselves when their brother died, so our responses to the physical place of the nave, and other parts of Durham Cathedral, will be influenced by our personality. And it isn't only personality that will influence our reading of the invitations to prayer that holy places offer and our responses to them. Our whole life story, including good and bad experiences in the past, and the context in which we find ourselves in the present, will all influence whether or not we hear these invitations and, if we do, how we hear them and how we respond to them. For example, it is easy to wonder, but difficult to imagine, what kind of holiness the Scottish prisoners found in Durham Cathedral when it became their jail in 1650, and what kind of invitation to pray it offered them. Whatever it was, it must have been very different from that experienced by tourists and pilgrims of the twenty-first century.

Life offers many invitations to pray – such as when someone we love dies, or when we meet someone (like Jesus in John's gospel) who seems to hold all the answers, or when we encounter a timeless, inviting place that simply seems to beckon us to stop and open our hearts to God. What matters is not so much how we perceive the invitation, or how we respond to it, but rather that we do take notice of it and that we do respond with integrity and from our hearts and minds.

When we walk into a holy place we become a part of it – as though we are ourselves new characters added to the narrative of the story that it tells. Our story, in a small way, becomes a part of the story of the place, and the story of the place becomes a part of our story. Each helps to interpret the other, for we are both the readers of these words and stories, and also ourselves a part of what is read. On the one hand, our personality and life story will lead us to 'read' holy places and their stories differently – for each person who arrives in a given holy place will find different things to read there, some of them very personal. On the other hand, our reading of the holy place also leads us imperceptibly into reading something about ourselves. Holy places help us to learn about ourselves as much, if not more, than giving us the opportunity to find out about them.

An Invitation to Pray

Holy places invite us to pray. In this chapter, I have explored some of the ways in which I think Durham Cathedral invites me to pray, and some of the ways in which that invitation may be experienced differently by different types of people. Other holy places may have a different vocabulary for their form of invitation (although I suspect that the vocabulary of holy places that we will encounter in this book actually covers most of the important words that they will draw from) but I think that all holy places have this invitation offering function in common. Particularly, the invitation is offered when and where we make our visit, but that is not to say that it ends there. The invitation can be extended to other times and places. In the next chapter we shall consider one of the ways in which it can be extended across time.

❦

Exploring Invitations to Pray

You may wish to explore God's invitation to prayer in Durham, or elsewhere. The following are just a few suggestions as to how you might begin exploring this invitation. Do not feel restricted by these suggestions, but take and use any ideas that appear inviting and leave those which do not. Such invitations may be explored by means of setting aside an hour or more on a single occasion, or else by setting aside a few minutes each day. They might be responded to by making a retreat or pilgrimage over a period of a day or more, or your response might take the form of making a quiet space at the beginning or end of the day, or during the course of a normal working day. Adapt the suggestions that are offered in this and subsequent chapters to suit the place that you have chosen, and the circumstances of your own life and daily routine.

In the Nave of Durham Cathedral

Spend some time sitting quietly near the west end of the nave, in the first bay between the pillars to the east of the main entrance. (Try to avoid the times of services that are being held in the nave or quire.) Allow your eyes and your thoughts to explore the building around you. What does this building say to you about the God to whose glory it was built?

Spend some time exploring some of the invitations offered by the stained glass in the north and south aisles. In the top panel of each of the windows in the south aisle, each saint holds an object of some significance, and in the lower panels two scenes from their lives single out things for which they might best be remembered. Remaining for a little longer where you are, spend some time reflecting on the windows visible from your seat in the first bay.

In the stained glass to your left are episodes from the life of Bernard Gilpin (1517–83, 'Apostle of the North' and Archdeacon of Durham), and to your right is the window dedicated to St Paulinus (Archbishop of York, d.644), who brought Christianity from Rome (via Kent) to the north of England in the early seventh century, and who was instrumental in the conversion to Christianity of the Northumbrian King

Edwin and Pagan High Priest Coifi. Edwin was baptized in 627, but was killed in battle in 633, after which Paulinus fled south. What does God call you to do, and to whom does he send you? God's invitations do not always appear to end well. In what ways have you responded to God only to feel that everything has fallen apart?

Move forward to a seat in the next bay of the nave. The south window in this bay is dedicated to St Aidan (d.651, Bishop of Lindisfarne). At the invitation of King Oswald, Aidan brought Christianity from Iona to the northeast of England in 635 and became the first Bishop of Lindisfarne. He died at Bamburgh in 651, but by this time he had proved himself an effective missionary and had trained others to continue his work after him. God's invitations sometimes come through other people, and God asks us to extend them in turn to others too. What invitations might God be giving you to offer to others?

Move forward again to the next bay of the nave, to spend some time reflecting on the window dedicated to St Cuthbert (635–87, Bishop of Lindisfarne).[20] One of the panels shows Cuthbert praying on Inner Farne. Cuthbert was an effective preacher and pastor, but his life was marked by his response to God's invitation to him to spend time in prayer, and this was his greatest love. How do you respond to that invitation – here or elsewhere? What is your greatest love?

Move forward again, to the next bay. This time, the window on your right is dedicated to St Benedict Biscop (628–89, founder and abbot of the monasteries at Jarrow and Wearmouth). Benedict was a patron of the arts and of literature. On his various trips to France and Rome, he brought back books, paintings, communion vessels, vestments, relics of the saints, traditions of Roman liturgical practice, stonemasons and glass-makers, all to enrich the life of the Church in England and more effectively to communicate the grace of Christ, both with those who were educated and with those who were not. Benedict worked tirelessly in order that the invitation that Christ offers might be communicated in new, varied and more effective ways. This cathedral offers to us today exactly the kind of invitation that Benedict sought to offer in his day. How do we respond to it?

Move forward again, to the bay that is situated at the front of the nave. The final window on the right is dedicated to St Bede (c.673–735, Doctor of the Church and monk at Jarrow and Wearmouth).[21] Bede was a scholar, encouraged by Benedict Biscop, who dedicated his life to communicating the grace of Christ in written words. He was a devout and thoughtful scholar of scripture, who invited others to reflect on God's revelation of himself to human beings in Christ. He continued work on a translation of John's gospel right up until his death. Reflect for a moment or two upon this passage from John's gospel, which also provides a link with the window visible on your left in the first bay of the north aisle, or else use one of the other passages from John's gospel quoted elsewhere in this chapter:

> I am the good shepherd. I know my own and my own know me, just as the Father knows me and I know the Father.[22]

Perhaps before you leave this place you may like to light a candle on one of the stands provided in this bay of the nave.

In the Nave of Durham Cathedral or Another Cathedral or Church

Explore the nave as a place of architectural and historic interest. Wander up and down the aisles, and around the area near the font. Observe the stained glass, the architecture, any memorials or tombs and other features. Find out something about the history of this place – perhaps from a guide, or guidebook, or from other literature or signs. Take your time, and do not rush. Feel welcomed here.

Pause for a few minutes somewhere near the door of the church. Where, within the nave, would you most like to sit or stand to pray? What would you most like to spend more time looking at? Move to one of these places (or perhaps they are the same place?) and sit, or kneel, or stand there for as long as you feel you would like to – but at least for another 10 or 15 minutes. Simply be aware of the presence of God in this place, and observe your surroundings. Don't force anything, but allow your surroundings to 'speak' to you. What do they say? How do you feel? What are the patterns of light and dark? What symbolism do you notice? What connections do these things make with life outside the Cathedral – your own, or that of other people? What invitation does the nave offer to you?

Respond in prayer in any way that feels appropriate – by lighting a candle (if facilities are available for this), by reading one of the prayers in this book, or perhaps by saying the Lord's prayer or another prayer known to you, by reading a passage of scripture, by making the sign of the cross, or by forming a prayer in your own words.

You may like to use this prayer for St Aidan's day:

> Everlasting God,
> you sent the gentle bishop Aidan
> to proclaim the gospel in this land:

grant us to live as he taught
in simplicity, humility and love for the poor;
through Jesus Christ our Lord.
Amen.[23]

Pause for a minute or two before moving on.

In Another Place

Thinking about the themes of this chapter, find a place which has some particular association for you with the offering and receiving of invitation, belonging to the body of Christ, or the coming of light into darkness, or which creates a sense of the vastness of space and of timelessness.

Spend some time in this place, simply becoming aware of your surroundings. What do you notice? If particular associations or symbolism become apparent to you, then reflect further on this. If not, simply be at peace in this place and be aware of the presence of God with you there. Are there other people in this place? What are they doing? Be aware that Christ is present with you in them.

Spend some time reflecting upon the first part of the prologue to John's gospel:

In the beginning was the Word, and the Word was with God, and the Word was God. He was in the beginning with God. All things came into through him, and without him not one thing came into being. What has come into being in him was life, and the life was the light of all people. The light shines in the darkness, and the darkness did not overcome it.[24]

Read the passage through several times. In what ways does your 'holy place' represent or communicate something of the presence of the eternal Word of God? What invitations does it offer you? How do they make you feel? How will you respond to them – both now, and when you leave this place? Offer your thoughts and plans to God by holding your open hands in front of you, or else in the words of a prayer.

After you have finished your prayer, pause for a minute or two in silence before moving on.

Chapter 4

Daily Prayer: The Quire and Sanctuary

If the nave of Durham Cathedral says something about the timelessness of God, I think that the quire says something about the presence of God in time. But time is a created thing, and God the creator is outside time – something that is very difficult for human beings to imagine. To talk about the presence of God in time is therefore to talk about the human presence of God within creation. In other words, it is all about the incarnation of God in Jesus of Nazareth. Of course, all of Christian thinking and practice is about this theme in some way or another. But in the quire of Durham Cathedral, God in Christ has been sought daily in prayer, on an almost continuous basis, for nearly a thousand years. There is something both humbling and comforting about praying each day in a place, and in a way, in which others have also searched for and found God over such a long period of time.

History

As was traditional, construction of Durham Cathedral began from east to west. This ensured that the places of the altar and Cuthbert's tomb were completed first, and thus that pilgrimage and liturgical use of the new building might begin as soon as possible. When construction of the present Cathedral began in 1093 the sanctuary and quire were thus the first parts of the Cathedral to be built. In 1104, construction of the quire was completed and the remains of St Cuthbert were transferred to a shrine at the east end of the new Cathedral.

The quire and sanctuary of the Cathedral were at the heart of medieval monastic life, in Durham as elsewhere. Originally, they would have been completely physically enclosed and inaccessible to outsiders. Eight times each day the monks would gather in the quire to sing the Divine Office:

Daybreak	Lauds
6.00 a.m.	Prime
9.00 a.m.	Terce

Midday	Sext
3.00 p.m.	None
Sunset	Vespers
Before bed	Compline
Night	Vigils (Matins)

All of these times of prayer were based primarily upon psalmody and were supplemented by scripture readings and commentaries, hymns, antiphons and responsories.

In between these times for prayer, the monks would have engaged in work around the monastery, study and, of course, sleep. Each day, thus, had a well-established rhythm, based upon the rule laid down in the sixth century by St Benedict[1] and centring upon the use of scripture, and especially the Psalms, for prayer.

Following the Reformation, and the dissolution of Durham Monastery in 1540, the rhythm continued, albeit with only two daily offices of Morning and Evening Prayer, but now as part of the new Cathedral foundation rather than as a part of a monastery. Only during the English Interregnum of 1649–60 has the daily cycle of prayer been neglected in Durham Cathedral.

Daily prayer was thus a priority in building the Cathedral, and it has permeated the life of the Cathedral ever since.

Physical Features

Although the quire remains fundamentally as it was 900 years ago, in the thirteenth century the Norman vault was replaced, having become unsafe. (Was it, perhaps, an experimental and innovative part of the architecture that was just a little too far ahead of its time?) Other changes since then, while not fundamentally changing the architecture, have influenced the appearance of the place more significantly.

At the eastern end of the quire lies the sanctuary. Behind the High Altar is the fourteenth-century Neville screen. Carved from Caen limestone, this screen originally provided a setting for 107 alabaster statues of saints and angels. The central statue was that of the Virgin Mary, flanked on either side by St Cuthbert and St Oswald. It is said that the statues were removed and hidden by the monks at the time of the Reformation, and it remains a mystery to this day as to where they went. Their absence provides a continuing reminder that all Christian prayer is joined with that of the whole communion of saints – visible and invisible.

The High Altar, with the Neville screen behind

Most of the cylindrical or semi-cylindrical pillars at the eastern end of the Cathedral, including the four visible in the quire, are decorated with an ascending anticlockwise spiral. This is said to be copied from those in the old St Peter's Basilica in Rome, which in turn were traditionally said to be taken from Solomon's temple in Jerusalem. The spiral draws the eye, and perhaps also thoughts, upwards towards heaven and may be thought of as symbolic of prayer.

On the south side of the quire, near to the sanctuary, is the colourful and imposing Hatfield throne, the seat (or 'cathedra') of the Bishop of Durham. Designed by Bishop Hatfield himself (d.1381), it is situated over his tomb at a height that is said to have made it the highest bishop's throne in Christendom at the time. It provides a reminder of the temporal as well as spiritual power that the Prince Bishops once held. There is a very positive place for being reminded that the Church, like all human institutions, flourishes when power is used well and is respected. It must also be true that if the Church exerts no power or influence in this world at all it will be because it is ineffective in its mission. So, why do I find myself struggling to see this beautiful feature as anything other than another reminder of the 'dark side' of the Cathedral?

Somehow, the Hatfield throne appears to me to demonstrate the hubris of a Prince Bishop who chose to emphasize the power of his position, and to grasp for himself a place of honour for his burial. This contrasts so greatly with the humility that Christ is recorded as having taught,[2] and that Cuthbert emulated, that it is difficult for me to imagine how Bishop Hatfield could have been so brazen. And yet, it serves to remind us how blind we can be to those parts of Christ's teaching that do not affirm the place that we feel we should be accorded in this world. Ironically, it is when we look down on

The Bishop's Throne with Bishop Hatfield's tomb beneath

Bishop Hatfield from our own sense of superiority, that we demonstrate just how much like him we are ourselves.

The current appearance of the nave is also influenced significantly by the dark carved woodwork of the seventeenth-century stalls, and the pulpit, introduced by Bishop John Cosin (1594–1672). The design of the woodwork reflects that of the rather more delicate stonework of the Neville screen. The Latin wording on the front of the quire stalls reflects the theme of praising God – especially with music and psalms.[3] Above and behind the stalls, on both the north and south sides, is the organ. The organ and choir, both with an international reputation, are capable of providing the most beautiful sounds, which fill the Cathedral and lift the human spirit. It is St Augustine who is attributed with having said that 'he who sings prays twice',[4] and there is no doubt that the musical tradition of the Cathedral contributes significantly to the overall sense of spirituality of the place.

When the Cosin screen was removed in the nineteenth century, thus opening up the western end of the quire to the nave, the effect was apparently very disappointing, making the Cathedral appear like a long tunnel. At its western limit the quire is now separated from the crossing and nave by the marble and alabaster crossing screen designed by Sir Gilbert Scott and installed in 1876. This screen incorporates a St Cuthbert's cross and an Iona cross, and shells (symbolic of pilgrimage) have been incorporated into its decoration. It thus draws together representations of the mission of Aidan, the ministry of Cuthbert, and the role of the Cathedral as a destination of pilgrimage. The structure of the screen is sufficiently open for the quire to communicate visually and audibly with the whole cathedral. Though the quire is separated as a place of prayer, it is still a part of the whole church.

The setting for daily prayer that the quire now provides is one of the most beautiful to be found in any cathedral or church in Europe. In the morning the rising sun lights up the Cathedral through the multicoloured glass of the rose window, visible high above the Neville screen, and in the evening the setting sun in the west creates patterns of light and shade which are projected onto the stonework of the nave, visible through Scott's screen. The empty niches of the Neville screen, and the representation of the apostles and elders surrounding Christ in the rose window, provide reminders that prayers offered here are offered in the company of all the saints and of the whole company of heaven. The Latin inscriptions on the quire stalls provide reminders that our purpose is to praise God, in music and with our voices, as well as in other ways. The Hatfield throne provides a reminder that our prayers are offered in the context of powers that influence the lives of human beings; political powers to order the world for good or ill, and dark powers of the human soul to deceive and serve itself rather than God. But mostly this is a place of light; light within darkness, light not overcome by darkness. Even worshipping in this place on a daily basis, it is hard to lose the sense of awe and beauty, and of the presence of the numinous, that it instils.

Daily Prayer

Morning and Evening Prayers continue to be offered each day in the quire. The morning liturgy is usually said – although Matins is sung on Sundays. The evening liturgy is usually sung. From Monday to Saturday the morning order is according to the Church of England's provision for *Daily Prayer*, a liturgy published in 2005 but based upon the pre-Reformation structure of daily prayer in the Catholic Church. On Sunday mornings, and every evening, the order is according to Cranmer's *Book of Common Prayer*, a liturgy that is one of the most beautiful and enduring products of the Reformation in England.

Sadly, by the time of the European Reformation, the medieval order of daily prayer had become primarily the province of monastic communities rather than of ordinary Christians. In the midst of the dangerous and confusing world in which the Church of England found itself at this time, Archbishop Thomas Cranmer (1489–1556) attempted to provide a form of prayer that could be used by all Christian people on a daily basis. He left a beautiful, simple, and profound liturgy, published first in 1549, that has stood the test of the almost half a millennium that has elapsed since. The 1662 revision, which remains in use today, is still largely composed of Cranmer's original prayers. As a member of the Church of England Convocation in 1661, Bishop John Cosin of Durham contributed significantly to the work of producing this revision of Cranmer's liturgy. Durham University library holds a copy of a 1619 edition of the *Book of Common Prayer* annotated by Cosin in advance of this task.[5]

Among Cosin's contributions to the 1662 *Book of Common Prayer* is his translation of the Latin hymn *Veni Creator Spiritus*, thought originally to have been written by Archbishop Rabanus Maurus (776–856). This hymn, included in the *Book of Common Prayer* for use at ordination services, was originally sung as a part of the rhythm of daily prayer. Cosin[6] included it in his own *Collection of Private Devotions* for use during the 'Third Hour' of the day (i.e. mid-morning):

> Come, Holy Ghost, our souls inspire,
> And lighten with celestial fire.
> Thou the anointing Spirit art,
> Who dost thy seven-fold gifts impart.
>
> Thy blessed unction from above,
> Is comfort, life, and fire of love.
> Enable with perpetual light
> The dulness of our blinded sight.
>
> Anoint and cheer our soiled face
> With the abundance of thy grace.
> Keep far our foes, give peace at home;
> Where thou art guide, no ill can come.
>
> Teach us to know the Father, Son,
> And thee, of both, to be but One;

> That, through the ages all along,
> This may be our endless song:
>
> Praise to thy eternal merit,
> Father, Son, and Holy Spirit.[7]

The offices of morning and evening prayer in both *Common Worship* and the *Book of Common Prayer* are based today, as in medieval England, almost entirely around the reading of scripture, and especially the Psalms. The Old and New Testament readings are governed by a cycle (or 'lectionary') that is used in common with other Christian denominations, and it provides a three-year programme for working through almost the entire Bible. This cycle of systematic reading of scripture is interrupted from time to time by readings based upon a yearly calendar of the Christian seasons (the *temporale*) and festivals of saints (the *sanctorale*), where the readings for the day are appropriate to the festival or season at hand. The psalms are recited on a monthly cycle, so that the Psalter is recited from beginning to end every month, again interrupted from time to time by the use of psalms appropriate to the *temporale* or *sanctorale*.[8]

In this way, the basis for daily prayer is a bringing of scripture into the rhythm of daily life, and a bringing of daily lives into the light of scripture. The effect is to increase familiarity with scripture and to provide a place within which there can be reflection upon what scripture says to us about the concerns and activities of our daily existence. It provides a basis for doing this within which we are encouraged first to turn to God and to listen to what he might say to us through scripture rather than first turning to the things that we are concerned with and the things that we want God to do for us. Within this daily pattern, different components of the liturgy – different holy places within the order of daily prayer – enable different concerns of prayer to be brought into focus one after the other.

There are lots of holy places within the order of daily prayer, but just four of them will be considered further here: the Prayer of One Heart and Mind, the psalmody, the gospel canticle, and the intercessions.

Prayer of One Heart and Mind

At Morning Prayer, near the beginning of the order provided in *Common Worship*, there is an optional prayer that seems to me to summarise the reason why we come to this place of prayer at all:

The night has passed, and the day lies open before us;
let us pray with one heart and mind.

Silence is kept

As we rejoice in the gift of this new day,
so may the light of your presence, O God,
set our hearts on fire with love for you;
now and forever.

All   Amen.[9]

It always seems a sadness to me when the person leading Morning Prayer (in Durham Cathedral or elsewhere) rushes through the silence that is integral to this prayer. Within this silence, the multitude of concerns that we bring to our prayers each day are focused into the unity of that one thing which is needful – the saving presence of the love of God in all our lives.

The metaphors of darkness and light, the ending of night and the beginning of day, allow us to entrust to God all of those things in our lives that are in need of his salvation, whether we know and understand them or whether they are bewildering, confusing or unknown. Praying with 'one heart and mind', we do not have to have resolved our differences or to have found solutions to the things on which we do not agree. We simply agree together, in the silence, that we submit to the way that God wants things to be, and that *this* is our prayer. Extending the metaphor of light to the kindling of fire, we then ask that God may increase our love for him in *this* day, whatever it might bring.

Sometimes, the silence of this holy place has seemed to me to say more about why Christians pray, more about why I pray, than all the multitude of words that we bring to our worship and life together. In the silence, we can trust God to insert the words that are needed for our prayers. In the silence, we do not have to know what to say –for we allow the eternal Word to be all that needs to be said. Sometimes, I have just wanted to stay in this place of silence. But this place is also deeply challenging. It can, or should, be a reminder of just how self-sacrificial true prayer can be. This is not just an abstract wish for unity – but an expression of willingness that I might be changed, and be an agent of change, in the cause of the unity that is God himself. And, of course, as our prayers continue, and as we go out into the world when the liturgy is concluded, we do have to engage our faith in Christ more specifically with all that is going on in our lives and in the world. Only in this way will the light of Christ finally dispel the shadows of darkness and set our hearts on fire with love for him.

Psalmody

At both Morning and Evening Prayer, there is a place for recitation or singing of the psalms. This ancient practice can seem strange at first, especially when (as in Durham Cathedral) the traditional method of recitation is adopted, leaving a brief pause in the middle of each verse[10]. The words have their original context in a world that is unfamiliar to us, a world in which things such as animal sacrifice, the worship of carved idols, and warfare involving spears and chariots were all commonplace images. When the psalms are sung by a choir, there is also always the danger for the congregation of being seduced by the beauty of the music and not paying attention to the meaning of the words. But for those who have ears to hear what is said, the Psalter is unique in giving expression to the full range of human emotion in such a way that it provides exactly the words that are needed to give expression to our deepest needs. Let us take just two psalms as examples of this.

When reading Psalm 56 in daily prayer, we do not need to be at war, or even to have enemies or adversaries in the literal sense of people who wish us ill, in order for it to be meaningful to us. Rather we become aware of all the thoughts, circumstances and people that we find opposed to the work of God in our lives. Take, for example, the opening six verses:

1. Have mercy on me, O God, for they trample over me; ♦
    all day long they assault and oppress me.

2. My adversaries trample over me all the day long; ♦
    many are they that make proud war against me.

3. In the day of my fear I put my trust in you, ♦
    in God whose word I praise.

4. In God I trust, and will not fear, ♦
    for what can flesh do to me?

5. All day long they wound me with words; ♦
    their every thought is to do me evil.

6. They stir up trouble; they lie in wait; ♦
    marking my steps, they seek my life. [11]

It is God's enemies more than our own against whom we are praying, although it is our own feelings that are given expression by the psalm. Thus, we may feel wounded by the words that others have spoken about us, and the trouble that they have caused us, and this may be the concern that we have in mind as we say the psalm. However, equally, we may find ourselves identifying with the psalm in terms of the thoughts within our own hearts and minds that set us against God: the self-indulgence, pride, or dishonesty that are enemies of all that we would like to be and of all that God calls us to be. The war in which we are engaged may just as much be within ourselves, as within the community or group to which we belong. And, if it is a conflict with others that concerns us in our prayers, that is not to say that we do not need to pray about the conflict within us as well. Where exactly is our true adversary? Is it the other person who has hurt us, or is it our own thoughts of self-righteousness, unforgiveness and pride?

Again, in Psalm 22, the images of people laughing at us (v. 7), of being surrounded by fierce bulls (v. 12) or dogs (v. 16), do not need to be taken any more literally than the obviously metaphorical images of being a worm (v. 6), or of being laid in the dust of death (v. 15). It is the feeling of being abandoned by God to which the psalm gives voice, and it offers a prayer that God will nonetheless be near at hand. These are feelings that most (surely all?) Christians find themselves facing at some point in life. The psalm is an expression of a search for God amid fears that he has abandoned us, and it is of course all the more poignant since it is the opening verse of this psalm that we find as the last words to be uttered by Jesus on the cross in Mark's gospel:

1.   My God, my God, why have you forsaken me, ♦
    and are so far from my salvation,
    from the words of my distress? [12]

The psalm is thus not only an expression of our own prayer that God will not abandon us, but is a place of reflection upon the sufferings of Christ and thus a place in which we can identify ourselves with his suffering on the cross. It is a recognition that when we feel forsaken by God, we can still trust in Him. And this psalm ends in a place of hope:

30.   He has saved my life for himself;
    my descendants shall serve him; ♦
    this shall be told of the Lord for generations to come.

31.   They shall come and make known his salvation,
        to a people yet unborn, ♦
        declaring that he, the Lord, has done it.[13]

In these and similar ways, the psalms may become our own prayers
– prayers about how we feel ourselves and on behalf of others who
struggle with difficult feelings or who rejoice in happier circumstances.

Gospel Canticle

A different canticle taken from Luke's gospel provides a central and
unchanging focus respectively to Morning and Evening Prayer, and to
Compline. These canticles are taken from the words of Zechariah about
his 8-day-old son, later to be known as John the Baptist (Lk. 1.68–79);
the words of Mary to her cousin Elizabeth (the mother of John the
Baptist) about her pregnancy with Jesus (Lk. 1.46–55); and the words
of Simeon in the Temple as he held the 8-day-old Jesus in his own arms
(Lk. 2.29–32). In different ways, each of these songs of gratitude to God
expresses something at the heart of the Christian belief of God's plan
of salvation for human beings brought to fulfilment in the incarnation
of Christ. In many ways they are an unlikely choice; they are perhaps
not the passages that we would first choose today as expressive of
what is at the heart of Christian faith. But, they are songs from scripture that bring the core belief of Christians in God's plan of salvation
in Christ into the heart of our prayers for others and ourselves in
God's world.

Thus, for example, when we pray at Morning Prayer that the child
(John the Baptist) might 'go before the Lord to prepare his way' and
that he might bring to all people knowledge of God's salvation, we pray
for ourselves and for all Christians that we too, like John, might be
messengers to others of the good news of what God has done in Christ.
And again, when we express confidence in the dawn of a new day as a
metaphor of God's taking us from death to life, we are praying about
all of those circumstances in our own lives in which we need the light
of God's truth and the freedom that it brings.

1.   Blessed be the Lord the God of Israel, ♦
        who has come to his people and set them free.

2.   He has raised up for us a mighty Saviour, ♦
        born of the house of his servant David.

3. Through his holy prophets God promised of old ♦
   to save us from our enemies,
   from the hands of all that hate us,

4. To show mercy to our ancestors, ♦
   and to remember his holy covenant.

5. This was the oath God swore to our father Abraham: ♦
   to set us free from the hands of our enemies,

6. Free to worship him without fear, ♦
   holy and righteous in his sight
   all the days of our life.

7. And you, child, shall be called the prophet of the Most High, ♦
   for you will go before the Lord to prepare his way,

8. To give his people knowledge of salvation ♦
   by the forgiveness of all their sins.

9. In the tender compassion of our God ♦
   the dawn from on high shall break upon us,

10. To shine on those who dwell in darkness and the shadow of
    death, ♦
    and to guide our feet into the way of peace.[14]

Intercessions

Finally, the saturation of the liturgy by scripture is interrupted by a space for intercessions that find their focus in the daily and present concerns of the world, the life of the Church in the world, and the needs of all Christians. It is this single exception to the otherwise total dominance of scripture as the basis for daily prayer that provides the crucial point of contact between the timeless prayers of the whole Body of Christ, the Church across all ages, and the time-bound prayers of those saints gathered together each day on earth. This is therefore the place in which the Spirit of Christ in scripture is mysteriously brought to be at work in and through the Body of Christ (the Church) in the world. This place is not where we start to pray, although it may be anticipated by us inwardly as we pray the psalms, and neither is it where our prayers end. The beginning and ending of our prayers is in God himself, revealed to us in scripture. Neither is it the climax of our prayers, for that is expressed in the gospel canticle as God's plan for the world revealed in Christ. But it is important, nonetheless, that our prayers are brought into relation to the daily concerns that we have in this world, and this is the place which is provided to enable that to happen.

Holy Places in Daily Prayer

The daily offices of Morning and Evening prayer thus provide a series of holy places in which we can find God, just four of which have been described very briefly here. These places are not geographical places at all, they are metaphorical places, but they are nonetheless places that may be found in the quire of Durham Cathedral, just as they may be found elsewhere. The daily life of prayer in the quire therefore finds continuity with the prayers of all Christian people and of the whole Catholic Church. It is a place in which God is daily to be found in Christ in scripture and in which our faith in Christ is engaged with the realities of our lives in this world.

In this way, it seems to me that the daily prayer that takes place in the quire takes place not in a holy place within a holy building, so much as in a liminal place, a contemplative place which is at once both a part of the time-bound world in which we live and also a part of the timelessness of God's eternal presence.

I feel enormously privileged to be able to come to such a beautiful and inspiring place each day. I am always glad to return to it after a trip away from Durham for work or holiday. But I knew something of this place before I first came to live in Durham, and I know it still when I am far from home. It is a place of daily contact with God in which the rest of life finds its reference and it is beyond geographical location.

Daily Prayer, Tradition, and Personality

Our understanding of daily prayer and our way of integrating it into our lives will be influenced by our personalities, as well as by the Christian tradition to which we belong. These are not unrelated considerations, for we may well have chosen or adopted a particular tradition that best suits our personality. Whatever our reasons for belonging to a particular tradition – evangelical, charismatic, liberal, Protestant, Catholic, Orthodox, or other – it will offer its own familiar form of daily prayer. The evangelical Christian is more likely to talk about their 'quiet time', which is more likely to provide a place for Bible reading and extempore prayer. The catholic is perhaps more likely to use a set liturgical provision such as the one that I have described here. These traditions are experiencing much more interchange of practices and ideas than used to be the case. Celtic daily prayer, for example, provides an approach that is now popular across traditional divides. However, it is still likely that there will be practices that have been encouraged within our own particular tradition or local church, and that other approaches to daily prayer will seem relatively unfamiliar or even completely foreign to us.

Most of us, whatever our personality type or tradition, find daily prayer difficult sometimes. Some may like the routine, but then get stuck in it until it becomes lifeless and restricting. Others may want to be spontaneous each day, but find it difficult to make the space available for this to happen. Prayer shouldn't simply be a routine obligation, but neither will it always feel spontaneous – whatever our personality type. Some will be anchored in the present in their prayers and others will have a future orientation, but prayer is both about being in the present and aware of the future, just as it must engage both our feelings and our rational minds.

The question of how to engage in daily prayer is thus all about preferences. Whatever we prefer, we cannot afford to neglect completely the approaches to prayer that we don't prefer. The art is to find a balance that allows us to take advantage of our preferences but still to find integration and expression of our unconscious as well as our conscious life. To do this is likely to require experimentation, respect for Christians of other traditions, flexibility and (at least sometimes) a willingness to tolerate that which we don't find easy. All of this is true of all prayer, and most of us can manage these things occasionally; it is managing them on a daily basis that presents the bigger challenge!

Cathedrals, like most other holy places, offer opportunities for a variety of experiences of daily prayer. I have seen people in Durham Cathedral who have (on a more or less daily basis) walked around the Cathedral, or simply stood quietly in it for a few moments. Others kneel or sit alone, and still others come together for Morning Prayer or Evensong in the quire. Interestingly, whether because of a love of music in the evening, or commitments to work and family in the morning, there are always many more people in the congregation at Evening Prayer than Morning Prayer. Whereas the latter engages the congregation vocally in psalmody and prayer, the former is very much led by the choir, leaving few words for the congregation to say or sing. These are therefore quite different experiences of prayer in a variety of ways. And the same Daily Offices can be a very different experience for different people, or for the same person on different days. For one person Evening Prayer might be an offering of prayer by the choir on her behalf. For another person it might be a place in which to engage contemplatively with the liturgy. For the same person Morning Prayer on one day might be a real struggle with tiredness and concentration, and on the next day a mystical encounter with God.

Our preferences amongst the variety of experiences on offer in a place such as Durham Cathedral are only partly about what suits our daily routine or our enjoyment of music in worship. They have to do with whether we like to pray with lots of other people, or just a few, or on our own. They are about whether we prefer to form silent, personal, prayers in our own minds, or to share with others in prayers that are written down, spoken out loud, and well tried over many years. They are about whether we prefer silence or words, stillness or movement, the visual or the audible, and so on. God hears all of these prayers. The question is, which ones am I most able to pray? Where is variety helpful and where is perseverance necessary? What will help me most to find God in the holy places of every day?

Silence

We have encountered silence in this chapter as a place within the liturgy of daily prayer, but it is an important factor in other ways too. Visiting a holy place and being there in silence, whether alone or with others, is quite different from when there is not silence. Silence can be comforting or disconcerting, welcoming or hostile, inviting or impenetrable, full or empty, musical or not, harmonious or discordant, but it is almost always meaningful. We live in a society that seems to be uncomfortable with silence, and which imposes sound upon almost every circumstance. Yet, in the silence, if we will allow him to, God speaks to us. In silence we can listen. In silence we are drawn into relationship with God. In silence, we can become aware of the holiness of places. In silence every place is potentially a holy place.

In the stained glass of one of the windows in the north transept of the Cathedral is a quotation from Gregory Nazianzen (329–389):

Thy attuning teacheth the choir of the worlds to adore thee in musical silence.

Daily prayer is about the encounter with this musical silence in our everyday lives.

Daily Prayer

Daily prayer is a challenge for all Christians. It can feel so demanding that we are discouraged from even starting, or we can feel so discouraged by failure that we give up maintaining the effort. Just as a love affair has to survive the transition from the excitement of that which is new to the routine of that which is familiar, so our search for God in prayer has to be able to move beyond the first encounter and the initial impact of a holy place to a way of experiencing every day (and every place) as holy. This will involve us in finding God amidst all the difficult emotions and experiences of life – sadness, anxiety, fear, incomprehension, jealousy, impatience, depression and anger – as well as amidst those which we feel are holy – such as joy, love, peace, patience, kindness and so forth. Holy places offer us invitations to find God not only on a single occasion, but as a way of life.

Exploring Daily Prayer

Daily prayer can be explored in many ways and in many places. It is certainly not necessary to come to Durham Cathedral in order to engage in such explorations, and neither is it necessarily the case that the offices of Morning and Evening Prayer will prove to be the best starting point for you. However, as with all exploration, you do have to start somewhere! The following are some suggestions for places and ways in which to begin.

In the Quire of Durham Cathedral

> Praise the LORD! Praise God in his sanctuary; praise him in his mighty firmament![15]

Come along to a service of Morning Prayer or Evensong. Don't rush in at the last moment, and don't rush off afterwards. Allow yourself time to take in your surroundings before the service starts and allow yourself space and time to reflect on it afterwards.

What were the points of resonance between the physical surroundings of this holy place and the holy places within the service? For example, how did the music (if it was at Evensong or Matins) reflect and give expression to your feelings? What features of the building did you find your attention resting on during the readings? (Don't let this stop you from paying attention to what was being read! Just use it as a question to help your reflections afterwards.)

The Latin quotations at the eastern end of each bank of choir stalls appear to be quotations from Sir. 44.1 & 6.[16] This passage (Sir. 44.1–15) is a hymn of praise to those who have gone before us in the faith, and especially to those who were brave, wise and prophetic. The Neville screen similarly invites us (even though its niches are now empty of statues of the saints) to remember that we are joined in our prayers by the whole company of heaven. Whose example of prayer, courage or wisdom do you look to as inspiration for your own daily life of prayer? Perhaps it will be a local saint – such as Cuthbert or Bede – but don't feel restricted in your reflections on this. Ask God to grant you the grace to follow their example in your daily life and prayers.

In the Quire of Durham Cathedral or in Another Cathedral or Church

Blessed be the Lord, who daily bears us up[17]

Go along to a service of Morning or Evening Prayer. Again, don't rush in at the last moment, and don't rush off afterwards. Allow yourself time to take in your surroundings before the service starts and allow yourself space and time to reflect on it afterwards.

What were the places within the liturgy in which you encountered God? What was the nature of that encounter? What were the points of contact between your life, and the needs of the world, and God's eternal purpose for the world in Christ? In what ways (if any) did the Psalms, or other passages of scripture, give expression to how you are feeling and to your present concerns in life? Offer these points of contact, these places of encounter, to God as your prayers.

The daily offices take time to appreciate fully. Newness and un-familiarity may allow us to explore some new place in which God may be found, or they may just prove to be confusing and off-putting. If you can, try to come along regularly, either for a few days in a row, or perhaps on a certain day each week, or perhaps even every day over a longer period of time. What new places have you come to appreciate within this daily place of prayer?

In Another Place

> Happy are those who do not follow the advice of the wicked,
> or take the path that sinners tread, or sit in the seat of scoffers;
> but their delight is in the law of the LORD, and on his law they
> meditate day and night. They are like trees planted by streams of
> water, which yield their fruit in its season, and their leaves do not
> wither. In all that they do, they prosper.[18]

You might like to try using the daily office as a basis for prayer at home,
or at work, or on the train on your way to work, or while sitting in an
open park or countryside.[19] However, there are many other ways of
developing a daily pattern of prayer that both provides structure and
also allows space for a more explorative and contemplative approach
to finding God in the routine of each day. For example, you might like
to try the following:

Find a prayer that summarises something that you would like to be
at the heart of your daily life. It should not be too vague, so that it has
no personal relevance or meaning, but it should not be too specific. So,
a prayer for loving Christ in others (if this is something that you feel especially called to or challenged by) is probably better than either 'being
a better Christian' or 'being patient with colleague X at work'. It should
not be either too long or too short. It might be drawn from prayers
written by other people, or it might be in your own words, but it should
reflect something that is important and personal to you, an aspect of exploring your life in Christ and of becoming all that Christ calls you to be.

For example, you might like to take a verse from the prayer known
as 'St Patrick's breastplate'. (Various verses of this hymn/prayer are
given elsewhere in this book.) Or you might like to use a prayer such
as the collect for purity:

> Almighty God,
> to whom all hearts are open,
> all desires known,
> and from whom no secrets are hidden:
> cleanse the thoughts of our hearts
> by the inspiration of your Holy Spirit,
> that we may perfectly love you,
> and worthily magnify your holy Name;
> through Christ our Lord.
> Amen.[20]

Try to establish a habit of praying your chosen prayer every day. It is probably best to try to find a given time of day at which you can pray this prayer – perhaps on your way to work, or at bedtime – but there are advantages to varying the time and place if you are the kind of person who can still remember to do this every day! At first, simply pray the prayer each day and be aware only of wanting God to make that a part of the rhythm of your life and your desire for him. However, over a longer period of time be aware of those different aspects of the prayer that come to your attention each day, and pay attention to the ways in which you find that your awareness of the prayer is changing.

For example, if you have chosen the collect for purity as your prayer, you may find that on a particular day, or over a period of time, your attention is especially drawn to the clause 'from whom no secrets are hidden'. This might then become a focus for thanking God that he loves you despite knowing everything about you – even the very worst things that you don't like about yourself – or it might become a focus for asking God to help you get to know yourself better. Something like this could then usefully become a focus for a quiet day or a retreat, but the intention here is not so much that that should happen as that this prayer should become a part of the fabric and rhythm of each day. Over time, you may well find that the emphasis changes again – either to a different part of the prayer altogether, or perhaps to a deeper level of reflection on the same theme – for example, to asking God to help us to accept those parts of ourselves that we try to hide from him, from ourselves or from others. However, these changes in emphasis should be allowed to happen naturally and in response to the questions that arise in your own heart. Don't try to force them to come.

Chapter 5

Praying on the Margins: The Galilee Chapel

Jesus came to Galilee, proclaiming the good news of God[1]

If God could be found in only one holy place, then that place would be defined for Christians by the life, death and resurrection of Jesus of Nazareth. This metaphorical place is historical, personal and particular. In fact, it is so particular as to be considered a scandal. How could God reveal himself so specifically in the life of just one person, in just one place, on the margins of the Roman Empire, at just one point in time? At least one important answer to that question is, of course, that God in Jesus is also present in the world in a very non-particular way. God does not reveal himself in only one holy place, but in every place.

If there was only one holy place in Durham Cathedral where Jesus could be found, then for me that would have to be the Galilee Chapel. Most obviously, as will be considered later in this chapter, that might be because of the name of the chapel or the objects within it that relate directly to the incarnation of Christ. However, more importantly, I think that it shares something of the quality of the gospel narratives that provide us with many bits of information about Jesus to think about and then leave us to reach our own conclusions about just who this man was. Pointers to the central tenets of Christian theology may be found in the accounts of the four evangelists, but it was left to other New Testament writers, and to the Christian Church of subsequent centuries, to work out exactly what the shape of this theology would be. Similarly, I think that the Galilee Chapel gives us pointers to our thinking about Jesus, but it leaves us with much of the work to do ourselves.

Finding Jesus in Galilee

Galilee is the historical and geographical place in which Jesus of Nazareth lived and went about during the period of three years prior to his death in Jerusalem. It is the place in which the accounts of the four canonical gospel writers have set most of the stories of his life, his teaching, his miracles and his various encounters with people prior to his death. It is also the place to which his disciples were sent after his death and resurrection as a place in which they would encounter him again. It is a place of encounter and re-encounter with Jesus.

The name 'Galilee' was probably conferred upon the Galilee Chapel in Durham Cathedral chapel because the processions at the Sunday services in the Cathedral would have begun and ended here. This was considered to be symbolic of Christ's journey from Galilee to Jerusalem, and thus to his passion, and the return of Jesus to Galilee after his resurrection. The name therefore symbolizes a place both before and after the passion and resurrection of Christ.

History

The Galilee Chapel was built by Hugh du Puiset (Bishop of Durham 1153–95). Work was begun in 1175, and it was completed c.1180–9,

The Galilee Chapel

about 50 years after completion of the nave of the Cathedral. It is recorded that building of a lady chapel originally began at the east end of the Cathedral, adjacent to the tomb of St Cuthbert, but that cracks began to appear soon after work began and that this was interpreted as a sign of disapproval of both God and St Cuthbert. This tells us something important about the psychological resistance of the monks to a new chapel that might have allowed women access to Cuthbert's shrine. But, whatever their motives may have been, building adjacent to Cuthbert's tomb was discontinued and the Galilee Chapel was built instead at the west end of the nave.

The location of the Galilee Chapel is highly unusual (although not completely unique). It encloses what would originally have been the Great West Door. After construction of the Chapel this huge exterior door became an interior door leading from a vast cathedral to a small chapel. The vastness of the door and the Norman arch in which it is hung, and the location of the Chapel (especially when viewed from the outside) provide a permanent reminder that this space is in a very real sense not inside the Cathedral at all. It is actually outside the west wall.

It is not only the location of the Chapel that is unusual. Being built on the narrow plinth of rock that remained between the original west wall of the Cathedral and the almost precipitous drop to the River Wear below, it is wider from north to south than it is long from east to west.[2] Inside, it is divided into five aisles, running from east to west, that are separated from each other by a series of four 'arcades', each comprising four Norman arches. In contrast to the huge pillars that dominate the nave of the Cathedral, these arches are supported by slender pillars, each of which was originally constructed of only two thin columns of Purbeck marble.[3] Windows in the north, south and west walls flood the chapel with light.[4] The overall effect of all of this is more reminiscent of a Middle-Eastern mosque than a European church. But its most striking feature was that it lacked the expected focal point of a single altar.

In fact, it may once have contained as many as 16 altars; more speculatively, it may have played a part in ceremonies concerned with the re-admission of penitents to communion. It probably functioned as a place that pilgrims would visit prior to going to Cuthbert's shrine. For a significant period of the history of the Cathedral, women were not allowed to approach the shrine itself, or even to pass beyond the line of black marble set in the floor of the nave just to the east of the present font. (One of the Durham Cathedral myths alleges that this rule was necessary because of Cuthbert's aversion to association with women, an aversion for which there is not only no evidence, but which is completely out of keeping with what we know of Cuthbert's pastoral sensitivities.) The Galilee Chapel was therefore the designated area in which women were allowed, and may have been a place in which monks could meet with their female relatives. It may be for these reasons, as well as its dedication to Mary, 'Our Lady', that it was also always known as the Lady Chapel.

Like other parts of Durham Cathedral, the Galilee Chapel has its 'dark side'. Fourteenth-century records refer to its use as a meeting place for the Bishop's Consistory Court,[5] a reminder that the worldly power of the Prince-Bishop was something to be feared as well as enjoyed. High above the Langley altar, over the Norman arch of the Great West Door, is an inscription in Latin: *Judicium Jehovae est. Domine Deus da servo tuo cor intelligens ut judicet populu' tuu' et discernat inter bonu' et malum* which, translated, means: 'Judgement belongs to Jehovah. Lord God grant to your servant an understanding heart that he might judge your people and discern between good and evil.'[6] It has also been suggested[7] that the Galilee Chapel, and its colourful wall paintings, may have been introduced in support of a rather worldly rivalry with St Thomas Becket's shrine in Canterbury. Pilgrimage may have been a spiritual venture, but it had important economic implications. And there may well be truth to the claim that Bishop Puiset was also trying to assert his claim as the rightful episcopal successor to Cuthbert and thus to reinforce his worldly authority and his prestige in the monastery. But it is not necessary to become entirely cynical. Puiset established a hospital for pilgrims, as well as building the Galilee Chapel, and there would not appear to be any need to deny completely his genuine charitable concerns.

A little more than two centuries after it was built, the condition of the Galilee Chapel had deteriorated. It was restored by Cardinal Langley (d.1437) in the early fifteenth century.[8] Langley also permanently blocked up the Great West Door by constructing a chantry altar in front of it, dedicated to the Blessed Virgin Mary. The Great Door being now blocked off, he constructed new doors providing access into the north and south aisles. After his death, Langley was buried in front of the new central altar that he had introduced.

Bishop Langley's alterations changed the impressions created by the Galilee Chapel in important ways.[9] It now has a central altar to provide a degree of focus, but there are many distractions from this amidst the aisles and arcades. It is no longer possible to walk in through the Great Door from the Cathedral, but access is still primarily from the east[10] rather than, as more usually in Christian churches, from the west. Among other things, this has the effect that one is immediately drawn in to the Chapel, and that it is necessary to turn to face an altar. But there is no single altar to turn and face. The Galilee Chapel thus immediately presents choices. Shall I come in? Where shall I sit, or kneel, or stand? Where shall I look first? Shall I merely pass through, or shall I stay?

This questioning, challenging, and ambiguity have not always been appreciated. In 1796 the Galilee Chapel was nearly demolished, but in response to a public outcry the plan was abandoned. If this chapel has provoked ambivalent responses, it has on balance evoked more affection than dissatisfaction.

St Bede

Although Durham Cathedral is best known as the shrine of St Cuthbert, who is buried in the feretory at its east end, here at the western-most end of the cathedral, in the Galilee Chapel, is the tomb of St Bede (673–735). It has been observed that the tombs of Cuthbert and Bede together represent an axis of goodness and truth within the Cathedral: Cuthbert's name being associated with goodness and holiness, and Bede's name being associated with learning and the pursuit of truth. Together, they represent the heart of what the Benedictine foundation of the Cathedral stood for.

Cuthbert (635–687) was revered for his life of holiness and prayer, and Bede's writings provide the major source of what is known about him. It was the presence of Cuthbert's tomb that made Durham a major centre of pilgrimage in medieval Europe. Healing miracles were said to be attributable to Cuthbert's intercessions, and Reginald of Durham, a monk in the late twelfth century, records a large number of healing miracles involving women in the Cathedral area, especially in the vicinity of the Galilee Chapel.[11] We shall give closer attention to Cuthbert in Chapter 7, where I will offer some reflections based around the part of the Cathedral in which he is buried. It is sufficient to say here that he was portrayed by Bede as someone whose holiness, prayer and miracles made him a Christlike figure: someone in whom Christ could be seen.

Bede was the foremost scholar in Anglo-Saxon England. He has become known as the father of English history but wrote also about the natural order of creation and other subjects. He compiled numerous commentaries on the Bible, which incorporated significant original thought as well as being based upon his scholarly awareness of the writings of Augustine of Hippo, Gregory the Great and others. But his life was dedicated first to prayer, and only secondly to learning. He entered the monastery at Wearmouth at the age of 7 years. Two years later he moved to the new monastery at Jarrow, and there he remained for the rest of his life. His life was therefore governed for well over 50 years by a daily discipline of prayer such as that described in Chapter 4.

Bede was originally buried in Jarrow, but his bones were moved to Durham in 1022. When the new cathedral was built, they were kept in the feretory in close proximity to Cuthbert's tomb. They were translated to a shrine in the Galilee Chapel in 1370. This shrine was destroyed by Henry VIII's commissioners in 1538 or 1539, during the course of the Reformation, and the bones were reburied in 1542. James Raine opened the tomb in 1831 and added the new cover with its inscription: '*Hac sunt in fossa Baedae Venerabilis Ossa*' ('in this tomb are the bones of the Venerable Bede'), an epitaph allegedly written with angelic assistance. Bede gained the title 'Venerable' within a century of his death and in 1899 Pope Leo XIII declared him to be a 'Doctor of the Church', a title recognising the value of his teaching for all Christian people.

The Venerable Bede was clearly not a scholar who pursued learning and knowledge as merely rational virtues desirable either for their own sake or in pursuit of some other utilitarian purpose. In the preface to his *History of the English Church and People*, he writes:

> if history records good things of good men, the thoughtful hearer is encouraged to imitate what is good: or if it records evil of wicked men, the devout, religious listener or reader is encouraged to avoid all that is sinful and perverse and to follow what he knows to be good and pleasing to God.[12]

His purpose then, in his writing, appears to have been the realization in human lives of that which is 'good and pleasing to God'. Like us, perhaps, Bede was also engaged in a search for God in holy places, and most especially in the holy places of the lives of the saints, for in them he found echoes of Christ. His *History of the English Church and People* even includes a third-hand account of the Holy Places 'of the sites of our Lord's Birth, Passion and Resurrection' which was only of very indirect relevance if we consider his task to have been purely one of a history of England. Its inclusion reflects his true Christological priority. Similarly, in his abbreviated version of the Psalter, he deliberately translates the Hebrew word for salvation as 'Jesus' in four separate places.[13] In two places he allows the text to refer to 'God our Jesus', in another (when addressing God) he refers to 'the joy of your Jesus' and in a fourth place he allows the text to say that God 'shall exalt the meek through Jesus'. We should not see these opportunities to speak about Christ as contrived, so much as reflecting his sincere search for God in Christ in holy places: geographical places, places in scripture, and places in human lives. Thus also, in his writing about Cuthbert, his intention seems to have been that, as this was a man who copied Christ, we ought to know about him. Here is someone (Bede was effectively saying) whom we would all do well to copy.

For Bede, Christ was the source of all the words of knowledge in which he had delighted in this world, and he was the fountain of all wisdom in whose presence this saint longed to be for eternity. This delight and longing united Bede and Cuthbert, in their different ways, and the presence of Bede's tomb in the Galilee Chapel is an important representation of what lies at the heart of the Cathedral.

Spaces Within Galilee

The atmosphere of the Galilee Chapel is one of intimacy. This is in contrast to the vastness of space encountered in the nave. The slender pillars in this chapel offer a feminine contrast to the huge girth of those in the nave. The nearness of its multiple arches emphasizes their curves, in contrast to the dominant height and strength of the larger arches of the nave. This feminine intimacy is womb-like. Not that this is a dark, confining place. On the contrary, it is light and open. But it offers a stillness, security and safety in which life may be found. It is a nurturing, protecting environment in which living reflections, thoughts and prayers may be conceived and come to birth.

Within this holy place, there are different spaces with very different characters.

Kneeling at the stall before Bede's tomb, in the inner-south aisle, it is the tomb itself which becomes the primary visual focus of the Chapel. In a chapel that is more than 8 centuries old, in the context of which a human lifetime seems such a short span of years, this is a moving reminder of human mortality. In the University City that Durham now is, Bede most obviously also reminds us of the value of learning, knowledge and wisdom. But in the texts that he left, examples of which are displayed boldly in carved wood on the east wall and more quietly in the calligraphy on the prayer stall here, Bede offers us more consolation than this. Wisdom and learning are to be desired because they emanate from Christ, whose presence is desirable above all other things. And it is in the ascended and glorified Christ that eternity lies. What we have seen of him in this world is just a promise of glory beyond all imagining, just as the glimmering of the morning star is a promise of the glory of a new sunrise.

At the east end of the inner north aisle lies an altar originally dedicated to Our Lady of Pity, which is currently the main altar of the Chapel. Behind this altar and high above the arcades are the remains of the medieval wall paintings that originally decorated this part of the Chapel. In the centre of the alcove behind the altar, where a statue or panel depicting Mary was originally positioned, there is now a large empty cross.[14] Seated here, the visual focus of the Chapel is provided by the altar and the empty cross behind it: symbols of the Eucharist and of resurrection.

In the very centre of the chapel there is a semi-abstract sculpture by Josef Pyrz, carved from ash, entitled 'Annunciation II'.[15] It portrays the Virgin Mary pregnant with Jesus. It is easy to imagine at first that this sculpture must be in the wrong place. Either it provides a distraction

The arches of the Galilee Chapel showing the medieval wall paintings, above

from the Langley altar, at the east end of the central aisle, or the triptych behind that altar[16] distracts from the sculpture. In either case, it
is difficult to know where to focus one's attention and it is easy to be
drawn quickly on before fully appreciating what either the sculpture
or the triptych has to offer.

In fact, the Chapel as a whole seems to provide a multitude of visual
stimuli, all vying for attention, each of which in turn distracts from
the others. In the southeast corner is the Last Supper Table, providing
a still-life representation of the bread and wine at the Last Supper,
all carved in oak. The stained glass provides abundant material for
visual contemplation and reflection. Older and newer glass variously
portrays Saints Aidan, Bede and Cuthbert, Hild, Oswald, Benedict
Biscop, Ceolfrith and others. There are representations of the Blessed
Virgin Mary, and Christ in his Galilean ministry. There is a lot going
on here. It isn't so much that the Pyrz sculpture is in the wrong place
as that this is visually an altogether busy place at the centre of which
the sculpture is to be found.

The outer north and south aisles are relatively empty, providing as
they do the primary ways in and out of the Galilee Chapel. It is quite
possible to walk in along one, to walk under the western-most arches of
the inner aisles, and then to leave again along the other without entering
the central space of the Chapel at all, and this is exactly what some tourists do. They pass through on the periphery without really engaging with
this holy place at all. They remain on the margins of this marginal holy
place and are not drawn into the intimacy of relationship that it offers.

The rich diversity of the Galilee Chapel contributes to its mystery.
The lack of one overall focus allows different foci of interest to come
to the fore in the different spaces within the overall space that is the
Galilee Chapel. Through history, it has clearly presented different faces
at different times. It continues to present different faces depending
upon the viewpoint that one adopts within its interior space. The
Galilee Chapel draws and questions and challenges. Like a kind of
sacred Rorschach inkblot, it offers the possibility of different interpre-
tations by different people at different times. From different places in
the Chapel different features of it are brought into visual juxtaposition,
thus creating different impressions and raising new questions. But,
within this diversity and ambiguity, can any unifying themes be found?
Is the interest of the Chapel merely that of the richness of a collection
of images that have been brought together over eight centuries, or can
something more be said about the ways in which God, and especially
God in Christ, may be found here?

I would like to suggest three strands of theological reflection that have shaped my own prayers here: one on the incarnation and passion of Christ, another on word and sacrament, and a third on the marginal, or liminal, nature of this place.

Incarnation and Passion in Galilee

Sitting at the back of the block of pews assembled in front of the altar in the inner north aisle, I have usually found myself drawn in my thoughts and prayers to the cross, the altar and the wall paintings. But from this place, two distractions from the central aisle have frequently 'intruded' upon my efforts to still my thoughts and focus my prayers. The first has been the beautiful carving of the annunciation to the Virgin Mary, who is portrayed holding the unborn child within her womb. The story of the annunciation is recorded in Luke's gospel:

> In the sixth month the angel Gabriel was sent by God to a town in Galilee called Nazareth, to a virgin engaged to a man whose name was Joseph, of the house of David. The virgin's name was Mary. And he came to her and said, 'Greetings, favored one! The Lord is with you.' But she was much perplexed by his words and pondered what sort of greeting this might be. The angel said to her, 'Do not be afraid, Mary, for you have found favour with God. And now, you will conceive in your womb and bear a son, and you will name him Jesus. He will be great, and will be called the Son of the Most High, and the Lord God will give to him the throne of his ancestor David. He will reign over the house of Jacob forever, and of his kingdom there will be no end.' Mary said to the angel, 'How can this be, since I am a virgin?' The angel said to her, 'The Holy Spirit will come upon you, and the power of the Most High will overshadow you; therefore the child to be born will be holy; he will be called Son of God. And now, your relative Elizabeth in her old age has also conceived a son; and this is the sixth month for her who was said to be barren. For nothing will be impossible with God.' Then Mary said, 'Here am I, the servant of the Lord; let it be with me according to your word.' Then the angel departed from her.[17]

Again and again I have found myself leaving my seat so as to read once more the poem displayed at the base of the sculpture:

Annunciation to virginity, yes
inscribed on life's blank page.
Virginity is not a relic of the past
for nothing passes,
but it is the very condition of our
　　existence.
Virginity is our present time.
As much as we are virginal
as much we are our very selves
opened on the world till we can holy be
　　seen through
as Mary is 'yes' comes from her purity
but purity is not our own selves
it is the symptom of our being alive
it is the door through which we pass
with closed eyes
the door of the Annunciation.[18]

Annunciation II,
by Josef Pyrz

I have pondered also on the abstract representation of the receptive furrows on the body of Mary and wondered what they might mean. I have gazed upon the face that accepted so great a privilege at such personal cost, to the point that it almost seemed as though the eyes might open and return my gaze.

The second 'distraction' has been the central panel of the triptych over the Langley altar. This distraction has been especially great, for it has seemed to me that it represented Christ's call to participate in his suffering and it has provided also a reminder of how little I have in fact had to suffer for him in comparison with his suffering for me. I have seen that the figures on either side of the cross – those of the Blessed Virgin Mary and St John – and the outline of the rocks in the background seem to outline a 'chalice' shape, within which the crucifixion is set. Did the artist, perhaps, intend an allusion to the gospel references by Christ to his passion as being the 'cup' that he had to drink?[19]

This painting has reminded me especially of meditations on the passion of Christ that I have undertaken while on retreat. This place is both where I deeply want to be – with Christ – but is also a place of which I am deeply afraid – for it challenges my comfort and security and self-interest. Often, I have identified myself with Mary Magdalene, hanging on to the foot of the cross. Like her, or at least like Mary as I have imagined her to be, I have found words in such a place completely inadequate as a means of prayer. Simply looking at the painting has become my prayer, for it represents God's presence at the heart of my own pain and struggle. So vivid has this image become that I can now see it, in my 'mind's eye', when praying elsewhere.

Sometimes, I have walked across and looked at the painting more closely. The panels follow from left to right: the procession of Jesus to the cross, his crucifixion, and then his being taken down from the cross and (as according to tradition) laid on the lap of his mother. Each of the key figures can be followed from one panel to the next, although St John does not appear in the first panel, and it is at times a little confusing to sort out which of the women is which. Without too much trouble, Mary the mother of Jesus and Mary Magdalene can be identified relatively easily in each of the three panels.[20] But who are the other figures? Painful scenes from all our lives can similarly become confusing and disorientating. At times we ask where our friends are. But always, perhaps especially at times when it feels as though God has deserted us, Christ is there.

Over time, various links between the painting and the sculpture crossed my mind. Both works of art are concerned with the theme of suffering. In the one Mary the mother of Jesus stands as a young woman, accepting the undeserved shame of pregnancy outside of wedlock and the prospect of the pain of childbirth, all out of obedience to the message of an angel and out of love for the child conceived within her. In the other she stands as an older woman suffering the pain of seeing the son whom she had loved so well cruelly and shamefully executed. However, it was a long time before I recognized the link that now seems to me to be the most important of all.

In the sculpture, the Virgin Mary's hands are placed either side of her own body, as though holding on to the new life within her womb. Words are not necessary to convey the pain and joy associated with the life-giving and creative event that has taken place within her. She simply holds on to the incarnate Word within her womb in hope and trust. But, in the painting, Mary Magdalene also simply 'holds on'. Clutching the foot of the cross, she hangs on in suffering and despair as the one whom she loved, and in whom she held such hope, suffers and dies. In neither representation is it necessary to employ words – although of course many words have been employed in an attempt to convey and interpret these events over two thousand years. The stillness and silence of these images conveys more powerfully what Christian life is all about than words can. At the most difficult times, when we simply do not and cannot understand, we are called to 'hold on' to Jesus. This is the heart of Christian prayer. Profoundly simple, but profoundly challenging, it is at times all that we can do simply to 'hold on'.

This is not to say that in prayer we will not also ask with words for salvation from the suffering and pain that afflicts us. However, if we are to be faithful to God, to allow him to bring to birth from within us that which is expressive of his deepest love for us, then it seems to me that we must be willing to follow Mary the mother of Jesus in being willing simply to hold on in faith and obedience. If we are to encounter the resurrected Christ, turning our deepest sorrow into our greatest joy, then we must follow Mary Magdalene in simply holding on to the foot of the cross, remembering that Jesus called us to take up our own crosses and to follow him.

Such 'holding on' prayers are simple, but very costly. They involve, for example, sitting in the Galilee Chapel – or anywhere – amidst our pain and fear, and without any immediate answers, but simply knowing that we are in the presence of Jesus and that this is all that matters. They involve continuing to be faithful to all that we believe to be good, even when we are aware of our own weakness and fallibility, and even when all seems to be lost and there is apparently no hope that things will get better. They involve saying 'yes' when those whom we love may misunderstand and when we know that the cost of doing so will make it feel as though a sword has pierced our hearts. They may simply involve our kneeling down and crying, not knowing whether our tears are for ourselves, or for others, or for Jesus himself.

Mary the mother of Jesus had the joy of giving birth to the Christ, and Mary Magdalene had the privilege of being the first to encounter the risen Christ. But we easily forget that these joys and privileges were at the cost of much pain. Holding on to the child in her womb, Mary faced the pain of an uncertain future. Hanging on to the foot of the cross, Mary did not know that the story would have a happy ending.

For me, these two images, representing the incarnation and the passion, provide an axis running through the centre of the Galilee Chapel from east to west. These central stories of the gospel – the Good News – of Jesus Christ are at the heart of what our prayers should be all about; they are at the heart of the experience of those who say 'yes' to God and who are obedient in following Jesus. They represent also the two major cycles of the Church's liturgical year: Christmas and Easter.

Perhaps it is worth recalling at this point that neither of the images that I have referred to here has been in its place in the Galilee Chapel for very long. Both were introduced in the twentieth century. However, the dedication of the Chapel to Mary runs back to the time of its build-ing, and medieval Marian devotion was very familiar with the pain of the sword that pierced Mary's soul.[21] Pilgrims hoping that Cuthbert might bring healing to them or to their loved ones would also have come to this place and prayed in hope for a miracle. It is a Chapel that must have been a place of prayer for those who were struggling in various ways for most, if not all, of its long life. And, of course, the stories of the incarnation and the passion that will have been told and retold here many times were also being told for more than a millen-nium before it was even built.

Ironically, neither the birth of Jesus nor the passion actually took place in Galilee. But, in Galilee, we encounter Christ incarnate. It is in Galilee that we decide to follow him – or not – and if we do it leads us to a sharing in his passion. That sharing in his suffering, in turn, takes us back to Galilee as the place in which we encounter the risen Christ. It is a place where our deepest needs meet the infinite power of God to raise even the dead to life. But it is a place also where we are challenged as to whether we will follow Christ even if it means that we will be treated like him.

Word and Sacrament in Galilee

If the incarnation and passion are a central theme in the Galilee Chapel, as represented by the triptych and the sculpture in the centre aisle, then they are still flanked by the altar dedicated to Mary on the north and Bede's tomb on the south. The impression created by these two parts of the Chapel, and the symbolism to be found in them, is very different. Doubtless the inner north aisle would have looked even more different when the wall paintings were complete and a statue or painting of Mary was still located in the alcove behind the altar. The inner south aisle must also have been very different before the translation of Bede's bones into it. But whatever the Chapel looked like then, the themes of incarnation and passion are not easily read into these spaces within the Galilee Chapel today.[22] The dates of the features found within them span from the medieval architecture and wall paintings, to a nineteenth-century tomb of an eighth-century saint and a twentieth-century cross. Reflecting on all of this, it is perhaps easiest to conclude that the Galilee Chapel is after all fragmented and diverse in its symbolism and that its atmosphere derives more from this diversity than from any coherence or overall unity. But, sitting and praying in this holy place, I have found myself contemplating the symmetry and balance that it provides.

The altar in the inner-north aisle is now the main altar of the Galilee Chapel. Sitting at the back of this aisle and contemplating my surroundings, the altar is a reminder to me that this is a sacramental space – that it is a place in which Christ's death is remembered, and in which bread and wine become his body and blood. In this sense, it seems to fit in well with the theme of the triptych over the central altar. It is, in a sense, another 'panel' that precedes the first panel of the triptych – reminding us of the Passover supper that Jesus shared with his friends the evening before he was to take up his cross. Like the triptych itself, this is not an entirely comfortable place to be. Sharing supper with friends is one thing. Knowing that it will be your last, and that one of your friends will betray you, is quite another.

In the inner south aisle, Bede's tomb provides a reminder that texts, wisdom and the search after truth have long been important in the Christian tradition. Notwithstanding the presence of a university in the city of Durham, this is not an emphasis on learning for its own sake. It is rather a reminder that words of scripture must be interpreted and reflected upon, and that this process often (although by no means always) itself requires the use of more words, as for example in the words of Bede's commentary on Revelation displayed here:

> Christ is the morning star
> who when the night
> of this world is past
> brings to his saints
> the promise of
> the light of life
> & opens everlasting day.

Words are important because they are able to lead us to knowledge of the Word made flesh, the eternal source of all wisdom.

There are mixed metaphors in this part of the Galilee Chapel. Christ is the morning star, who brings a promise of everlasting day. But in the words of Bede's prayer, with which he concluded his *History of the English Church and People*, and which is displayed on the stall at the foot of his tomb, Christ is also the fountain of all wisdom:

> I implore you, good Jesus,

that as in your mercy you
have given me to drink in
with delight the words of
your knowledge, so of your
loving kindness you will also
grant me one day to come to
you, the fountain of all
wisdom, and to stand for ever
before your face. Amen.

Both these metaphors, star and fountain, refer to the ascended and glorified Christ who reigns in eternal glory. They point us beyond the suffering of the triptych, reminding us that after death Christ invites his saints to share with him in everlasting life. Unlike the triptych itself, this is a more hopeful place to be, but of course it is not where we find ourselves just yet. It is a promise of something that is yet to be. It is something to look forward to amidst the pain and uncertainty of life in this world.

There is thus a symmetry about the Galilee Chapel in two dimensions. The central east-west axis of incarnation and passion intersects with a north-south axis of sacrament and word. This north-south axis is pivoted in time around our inhabitation of the present moment in time. As we share the Eucharist, we are participating with Christ in his passion – even though that is historically a past event. As we search for the truth of the Word incarnate we look forward to the promise that he makes to his saints that they might be in his presence forever. Both sacrament and word bring us into the presence of Christ, the Word made flesh.

The north-south symmetry in the Galilee Chapel is also expressed in at least one other way. In comparison with the central and inner south aisles, the inner north aisle feels very ill defined. A plain cross, an empty altar and wall paintings that are now so badly damaged and faded as to be impossible to decipher clearly[23] somehow feel very empty. The symbolism is implicit, but it is ambiguous and invisible. The bread and the wine on the altar, and the body and blood of Christ on the cross, are in fact not there at all – unless of course one is present at a time when the Eucharist is actually being celebrated. The inner south aisle is very different to this. Its symbolism is just about as explicit as it can be. Bede's tomb is a blunt reminder of human mortality. The words on the wall are symbols too. Words are very explicitly defined symbols indeed, conveying just about as positive and specific a meaning as human beings have found themselves able to represent. Bede was, in his time, skilful in the use of these symbols and he left us beautiful, illuminating and profound arrangements of them.

In the inner north aisle, then, we have an almost empty space, within which we are reminded that God is invisible and beyond all human portrayal. We are left with our own thoughts, which so often feel to us to be hugely inadequate and feeble attempts to seek after a God who is infinitely beyond us. Words fall away and we are left in the silence of the divine presence, a presence that is infinitely beyond all words. This invites contemplative prayer – which we shall discuss further in Chapter 7. But in the inner south aisle we find a reminder of the beauty and power of words. This is a space within which we are reminded that God has made himself known in the Word made flesh. This space invites us to respond in words – as Bede did. It invites us, for example, to the kind of prayer that we considered in Chapter 4.

This symmetry is a north-south axis of a very different kind. It reminds us that the incarnation and the passion of Christ are manifestations of an infinite God within time and space and that, as such, they must always be full of contradictions. The God who is fully known in the humanity of Christ is also the same God who is infinitely greater than human minds can ever be able to grasp. The God who reveals himself as the eternal Word is far above and beyond all that words alone can adequately convey. The gospels point us to Christ, and communicate Christ to us in words, but in silence we find ourselves in the eternal presence of the Word beyond all words.

In this way, the Galilee Chapel offers balance and harmony. It invites us to stop and think and pray, but when we do so it questions and challenges and confronts us. We are drawn by it into the incarnation and passion of Christ. His humanity is a participation in our humanity. Our suffering becomes a participation in his suffering. We are bidden to hold on to his presence within us, and to hold on to the cross of his suffering for us. This presence and suffering may be interpreted with words, and we are encouraged to seek his truth to the fullest extent that they allow, but we are never allowed to imagine that this alone will convey the fullness of God to us. With words, and in silence, we are simply encouraged to hold on to him.

Galilee as Marginal Space

The Galilee Chapel is an ambiguous and paradoxical place.

For many female pilgrims in the middle ages, the Galilee Chapel would have been the destination of their pilgrimage, their access to the shrine of Cuthbert itself being denied by the men who were its custodians. This is deeply ironic. Did those who named this Chapel not stop and reflect that Galilee was the place to which Mary Magdalene – a woman – was instructed by the risen Christ to send the male disciples that they may encounter him too? Did they not reflect that it was in a woman's womb that he became incarnate, or that it was women who remained with him at the cross? Did they not reflect that Christ was happy to be criticized for allowing women – even sinful women – to draw close to him?

Of course, it is easy for us to see the foolishness of this from the perspective of eight centuries, but it would be more foolish of us not to recognize the same blindness within ourselves. In pushing women to the margins of medieval pilgrimage in Durham, I wonder whether men did not ironically shift the spiritual centre of the Cathedral to the opposite end from the one that they intended. In the Galilee about which we read in the gospels, Christ always had time for those who were marginalized – be they men, women or children. And, given half a chance, we also marginalize those with whom Christ wants to be present.

The statue of Mary in the centre of the Chapel is a reminder that Christ comes to dwell with those on the margins. Mary and Joseph were poor citizens living in an occupied country on the margins of the Roman Empire. In her pregnancy outside of marriage Mary suffered disgrace and must have known what it was to suffer marginalization within her own culture and amongst her own people. Pyrz portrays Mary as a young African woman, reminding us that Christ is still born amongst the poor in the so-called developing nations of our world. At Christmas, we remember that Mary's child represents God's marginalization of himself from his own divine glory and power so that he might be 'with us'.

At Easter, when we remember the passion, we find ourselves drawn into the scene portrayed by the triptych. This is also a marginal place, a place of the margins of what we can bear, and a place of confrontation with the margins of life. It is a place of tears. We know that on Easter morning our tears will be turned to joy. But we have to imagine what it would have been like for the figures at the foot of the cross, confronted with loss of hope and overwhelmed by grief. For them, there was no assurance of a happy ending. All that they had hoped for had come to an end.

For one of the characters portrayed in the triptych, Mary Magdalene, tears at the place of the cross were to be followed by tears at another holy place – the empty tomb. During the weeks of the Easter season a model Easter garden, complete with its empty tomb, is usually on display in the Galilee Chapel, reminding us that Galilee is the place of encounter with the risen Christ. But this encounter occurs only amidst the tears of confusion and loss that are shed by those who share lovingly with Christ in this place of his marginalization in suffering and death. It is here that we are most intimately with him, and yet most painfully feel that we have lost him. Saint Anselm (1033–1109), in a prayer addressed to Mary Magdalene, reflects upon the tears that she shed at this holy and confusing place immediately prior to her encounter with the risen Christ:

> what can I say, how can I find words to tell,
> about the burning love with which you sought him,
> weeping at the sepulchre,
> and wept for him in your seeking?
> How he came, who can say how or with what kindness,
> to comfort you, and made you burn with love still more;
> how he hid from you when you wanted to see him,
> and showed himself when you did not think to see him;
> how he was there all the time you sought him,
> and how he sought you when, seeking him, you wept.[24]

The Galilee Chapel invites us, in its silence, its symbolism, its ambiguity and marginality, simply to be with God. In our sadness it offers comfort and in our joy it does not allow us to forget our pain. When God feels distant, it reminds us that he is present. When God feels close at hand, it reminds us of the alienation that God experienced within himself, in Christ, that we may know his presence with us. But, in providing us with a holy place in which to be with God, it does not allow us to forget others. It reminds us that when we marginalize others we may simply be distancing ourselves from those in whom we might meet Christ ourselves.

Praying on the Margins

Holy places are sometimes marginal. God is not always to be found at the 'centre' of what is going on, at least not according to human estimations of where that centre is. But, for Christians, God is supremely revealed in the life, death and resurrection of Jesus of Nazareth. Marginal places, places of rejection by religious authorities, places despised in human estimation, and places of crucifixion and pain, will therefore always be places in which Jesus is found. They will always be especially holy places. They will also, often, be the places in which we are most challenged in our search for God. They will often be confusing and disorientating. 'Distractions' will prove to be pointers towards God, and things that we thought to be central will prove to be peripheral. They will test our true depth of desire to find God. Do we still want to find him if it means being 'lost' in the estimation of our peers? Do we still want to find him if it leads us to tears, pain and loss of hope?

Holy places are places in which we find Jesus.

Exploring Prayer on the Margins

Praying on the margins can be painful and hard, but it is here – at the limits of our own ability to cope and on the margins of human society – that Christ calls us most especially to pray. Happily, the Galilee Chapel is a safe and welcoming place to pray, but that is not to say that it will not lead us to reflect on our own inner pain, or that it will not remind us of our calling to pray for those who are in less pleasant places. Nor are the following suggestions for prayer confined to those that may be offered in this place. But, perhaps, praying here may help us to pray in, and for those who are in, less comfortable places. Some of the proposed explorations of prayer may be challenging or unsettling. If you feel that you need to do so, you may like to discuss them with a spiritual director, a priest or pastor, or a friend. If you are praying in Durham Cathedral, you may wish to speak to a member of the listening team, or to one of the chaplains on duty. However, they are intended primarily as a means of bringing things that concern us, and cause us pain, into the context of the incarnation, death and resurrection of Christ. Be aware of his presence with you, and allow your pain to be a sharing in his. Allow him to draw you into a sharing in the hope and life of his resurrection.

In the Galilee Chapel
In the fourth century, Christians went literally to the margins of society, to the Syrian and Egyptian deserts, to devote their lives to prayer. Amongst those Desert Fathers and Mothers, as they became known, was a man called Macarius.

Some brothers asked Macarius, 'How should we pray?' He said, 'There is no need to talk much in prayer. Reach out your hands often, and say, 'Lord have mercy on me, as you will and as you know.' But if conflict troubles you, say, 'Lord, help me.' He knows what is best for us, and has mercy.[25]

Simple prayers, such as that which Macarius recommended, can often say more than complex and lengthy prayers, especially when we are at the margins of our own ability to cope.

Before going into the Galilee Chapel, spend some time outside the Cathedral, perhaps sitting in the cloister or else on Palace Green, reflecting on your present concerns in life: the things that cause you pain, anxiety or fear, and the other people for whom you are concerned. What is it that worries you most? What threat do these things present to you or to others? What do you most desire, for yourself or for the others about whom you are concerned? What are your worst fears? Having clarified in your own mind (as much as you can) what these things are, then mentally gather them together and use the Jesus Prayer as a means of bringing these things to God:

Lord Jesus Christ, Son of God, have mercy on me a sinner.

If you prefer you may use another simple and repetitive prayer, or an abbreviation of this prayer: e.g. 'Lord have mercy'. Choose something simple which can be repeated easily and from heart as a means of stilling your mind and focusing your thoughts on God. When you feel ready to do so, make your way into the Galilee Chapel.

Find a place to sit, or kneel or stand, in which you can see both the painting over the Langley altar and the statue of the annunciation. Allow yourself time to look at and reflect upon both works of art. What do you see? How do you imagine the various figures represented in these works of art might feel? What is happening? What symbolism do you find? Do you identify with one of the figures gathered around the cross? If so, which one? Or perhaps you identify more with the portrayal of Mary receiving the annunciation? What is it that you identify with? What are the possibilities for Christ to be born into the midst of your needs? What are the possibilities for resurrection? Can you believe in these possibilities? What would they mean in practical terms, and how would you be aware of them if they were to be real-ized? Whether or not you can believe that these things might actually happen, be still – with the figures around the cross, and with Mary. Let them become your prayer for Christ to bring his life into your life and into the lives of those for whom you pray here.

Before you leave, go to the prayer stall at Bede's tomb (if you are not already there) and pray the prayer of Bede that is written there. Read the inscription on the wall. Perhaps things still seem very dark? Be aware that Christ is your morning star – even if he currently only feels like a very small pinpoint of light amidst a very dark sky.

In the Galilee Chapel or Another Cathedral or Church

Now when Jesus heard that John had been arrested, he withdrew to Galilee. He left Nazareth and made his home in Capernaum by the sea, in the territory of Zebulun and Naphtali, so that what had been spoken through the prophet Isaiah might be fulfilled: 'Land of Zebulun, land of Naphtali, on the road by the sea, across the Jordan, Galilee of the Gentiles – the people who sat in darkness have seen a great light, and for those who sat in the region and shadow of death light has dawned.'[26]

Stand on the margin of the chapel or church – perhaps just inside a door, or at the western end. If you are in a cathedral other than Durham, find a side chapel or other place that is on the margins of the cathedral. Allow yourself a few minutes to survey the scene before you. Do you feel that you are within the cathedral, or on its margins, or even outside it? What choices are you confronted with? Where do you feel most drawn to sit or kneel to pray? Why does that place appeal to you?

Move to the place that you have chosen and sit or kneel there for a little while. Pay attention to your surroundings. Pay attention to how you feel – in body, mind and spirit. What do you see, hear or feel that is comforting? What is discomforting? What needs, anxieties, wounds or heartfelt causes do you bring with you to this place? Remember that many people in need will be likely to have prayed here before you – perhaps over many centuries. Be aware that God is present here with you in your need.

What features in your surroundings do you feel represent in some way how you feel within? Let these things – be they works of art, symbols, shadows, reflections, candles or other objects – be representative of your prayer. Perhaps there will be a postcard or guidebook that you can take away that will provide a reminder of this prayer. Or – if photography is allowed – you may wish to take your own photograph. Allow yourself time simply to be in this place and to reflect on what it is that you see (and hear, touch, etc.) and what it means for you.

When you feel that this time of prayer has come to an end you may wish to make the sign of the cross, or perhaps say a brief prayer that is well known to you – such as the Lord's Prayer – to mark the end of your prayers in this place on this occasion. However, as you leave, be aware that you leave your prayers in this place in the presence of God and that, in a real sense, they endure even after you have turned your attention back to the other affairs of life. You may then want to return here from time to time to take up these prayers again – but if you do, do not expect things necessarily to be the same each time. Different things may take your attention, and different concerns may be in your heart. Allow God to direct this time of prayer as he chooses – even if sometimes it is simply being still in his presence without any clear focus at all.

In Another Place

Give some thought to the marginal or liminal places in which you might pray – both metaphorically and literally. So, for example, you might give thought to praying for refugees, for the poor or homeless, for the areas of your own life in which you feel at the limits of your ability, or else for yourself or others at times of transition – leaving home, getting married, giving birth, or nearing death. Alternatively, you may know literally marginal places in which you can pray – overlooking your home town or city, on train or car journeys, being on the edge of a large crowd, on a sea shore, or in a deserted or remote place.

In your prayers in these places, or for these groups of people, you might find it helpful to reflect on some relevant passages of scripture, including perhaps one of the passages above, or else the following:

Meanwhile, standing near the cross of Jesus were his mother, and his mother's sister, Mary the wife of Clopas, and Mary Magdalene. When Jesus saw his mother and the disciple whom he loved standing beside her, he said to his mother, 'Woman, here is your son.' Then he said to the disciple, 'Here is your mother.' And from that hour the disciple took her into his own home. After this, when Jesus knew that all was now finished, he said (in order to fulfil the scripture), 'I am thirsty.' A jar full of sour wine was standing there. So they put a sponge full of the wine on a branch of hyssop and held it to his mouth. When Jesus had received the wine, he said, 'It is finished.' Then he bowed his head and gave up his spirit.[27]

Nicola Slee has written a prayer which reminds us that this marginal place, the place of the cross, challenges us about our ability both to hold on and to let go:

When we stand in the place of death and loss,
   Mary, stand with us,
   and teach us how to endure.

When we stand in the place of powerlessness, unable to act,
   Mary, stand with us,
   and teach us how to hold fast.

When we stand in the place of separation,
   Mary, stand with us,
   and teach us how to let go,
   releasing ourselves and all for whom we yearn
   into the mystery of divine love,
   so that we may become ready to move on
   into the new community of love where God's Spirit calls.[28]

How does it feel to pray in such places and for such people? In what way does Jesus make himself known to you or to others in these places?

Chapter 6

Pilgrim Prayer: The Chapel of the Nine Altars

The Chapel of the Nine Altars surrounds the feretory – the location of Cuthbert's tomb and the destination of pilgrims. It is therefore, by definition, a peripheral place. It is not even so much a 'place' as a part of a pathway around the east end of the Cathedral. It is a way of getting from the east end of one quire aisle to the east end of the other. In fact, for some visitors, who climb the stairs to Cuthbert's tomb from the end of one quire aisle, and who then descend the steps on the other side into the other quire aisle, it is neglected almost completely.

The Chapel of the Nine Altars is seemingly littered with memorials, coffins, stone carvings, sculptures, an icon, and other artwork, all of which appear to be more or less haphazardly arranged. Visitors move from one item to another, as though 'joining the dots' in a child's puzzle book. Arriving in the Chapel from one quire aisle, they leave it by the other, departing as though headed for the next numbered 'dot' somewhere else in the Cathedral.

The shape of the Chapel is a problem. It has open, almost square, spaces at each end, which provide northeast and southeast transepts to the Cathedral, with a narrow connecting corridor sandwiched between the east wall and the feretory. The Aidan altar is central, but is a constricted point of focus. Like the Galilee Chapel, this Chapel offers many distractions. Unlike the Galilee Chapel, this is not a space that draws the visitor inwards. Rather, the visitor is drawn from one end to the other. And, at each end, there is a space into which one emerges, but without the satisfaction of finding there any clear sense of order, destination or purpose.

The Chapel of the Nine Altars could be mistaken, at least in its north and south transepts, for a slightly untidy art gallery. True, there are some works of art here that are very beautiful indeed, and perhaps this mitigates all of the criticisms that I have made. But this chapel can feel as though it only offers stopping points at which to pause briefly for reflection along the way from one place to another place.

Of all the places in Durham Cathedral that I have been drawn to sit and kneel and pray in, this was for a long time one that I visited least often. Usually I would go here if other places were too noisy or busy, or simply if I wanted a change. However, having made an effort to visit it more often and to use it as a place in which to pray, rather than simply pass through, I have come to appreciate it very much. More work is needed here, but if that work is invested it will be repaid.

History

The original east end of the Cathedral comprised three apses, which by the thirteenth century were in a dangerous state. The central apse enclosed Cuthbert's shrine within a very confined and intimate space indeed. As numbers of pilgrims grew, this became impractical. Perhaps also there was a sense that so great a servant of Christ should be surrounded by a still more splendid building. This sentiment would have been deeply opposite to Cuthbert's own sense of humility and his seeking out of wild and remote places in which to pray. Regardless of this, between 1242 and 1280, the east end of the Cathedral was greatly expanded, to create what we now know as the Chapel of the Nine Altars.

The work was set in motion by Richard le Poor (Bishop of Durham 1229–37), whose architect was Richard of Farnham. In contrast to the Norman style of the nave and quire, the Chapel of the Nine Altars is an example of early English Gothic architecture, based on the design of the east transept of Fountains Abbey.

The work was paid for by the sale of indulgences. Ordinary Christians, hoping to obtain forgiveness of their sins and to reduce the time that they or those they loved would spend in purgatory, gave money to the Church for the purpose of building this chapel. In theory, this was a tangible expression of thanks for spiritual benefits bestowed graciously by God. In the eyes of Protestant reformers, it was an attempt to buy something that cannot be bought – the grace of God. It is hard for us to identify with this today, whether we be Catholic or Protestant: the combined effects of the Reformation and the Enlightenment have left us all with an impoverished sense of the connection between faith and works. This chapel was built in a world in which that connection was tangible and unquestioned, and in which financial and spiritual values were not so easily dissociated from each other as they are now.

The Chapel gains its name from the nine altars that originally stood along its east wall. These would have enabled the numerous priestly members of the medieval monastic community each to celebrate Mass on a daily basis. From south to north, the medieval altars were dedicated to:

- St Andrew & St Mary Magdalene
- St John the Baptist & St Margaret
- St Thomas of Canterbury & St Catherine
- St Oswald & St Lawrence
- St Cuthbert & St Bede
- St Martin
- St Peter & St Paul
- St Aidan & St Helen
- St Michael the Archangel.

The original, fifteenth-century, stained glass must have been dramatically beautiful. The themes of the nine tall windows in the east wall were related to the respective saints whose altars were immediately below. Above these was a large rose window. The window in the south wall depicted scenes from the life of St Cuthbert. The window in the north wall was a:

> goodly fair great glass window called Joseph's window the which has in it all the whole story of Joseph most artificially wrought in pictures in fine coloured glass.[1]

All of the windows have been reglazed, mostly in the eighteenth or nineteenth century, some of them with themes similar to the originals. Thus, the north window today shows a sequence of 20 scenes portraying the story of Joseph as related in the book of Genesis, but the south window is now clear glass and no longer tells its story of Cuthbert in glorious colour.

The nine tall windows in the east wall, from south to north, now portray:

- Saints Peter and Paul[2]
- Scenes from the life of John, the beloved disciple[3]
- Three scenes around a theme of the temple in Jerusalem[4]
- A series of scenes in the three central windows, portraying the life, passion and burial of Jesus[5]
- A series of scenes in the three northern windows on the theme of Christian discipleship.[6]

The rose window shows Christ enthroned in glory, surrounded first by the 12 apostles, and then by the 24 elders of the book of Revelation.[7]

In the northeast transept stands a marble statue of Van Mildert by John Gibson, a leading Victorian sculptor. Van Mildert (d.1836, Bishop of Durham 1826–36) was the last Prince-Bishop and was founder of Durham University in 1832.

The nine original altars have all been removed, but during the twentieth century three new altars were introduced:

- At the end of the south quire aisle, an altar dedicated to St Margaret of Scotland. Next to this is a picture in pastels of Margaret with her son, David, by Paula Rego.
- The central altar, dedicated to St Aidan, is decorated by a colourful frontal and reredos, which incorporate symbols of St Aidan, St Cuthbert and St Bede and of the flora and fauna of the northeast that these saints would have known, especially of Holy Island.
- At the end of the north quire aisle, an altar dedicated to St Hild. Next to this is an icon by Edith Reyntiens (1998), with a border depicting various scenes from the birth, life and death of St Hild.

This change is very significant. The 'Chapel of the Three Altars' speaks of local saints, and of early English and Scottish as well as Roman Christianity. It speaks to the part that women, as well as men, have played in the life of the Church.

Also during the twentieth century, a large pietà by Fenwick Lawson, in beech and brass (1974–81), was placed in the southeast transept. This larger-than-life representation of Mary and Jesus provides a strong visual and spiritual impact even in a building which already has a strong impact of its own.

Pilgrim Space

Four features combine to make the Chapel of the Nine Altars distinctive and together they create the character of the environment that it provides for prayer. These are its illumination, its height, its unusual floor plan, which is shaped by the pilgrim destination of the tomb of Cuthbert, and its stained glass.

Illumination

It is so obvious as to be easily overlooked that this Chapel is at the extreme east end of Durham Cathedral. Christian churches are traditionally arranged so that the altar is situated at the eastern-most end, and Durham Cathedral is no exception. The symbolism of this supports various explanations. In Matthew's gospel, Christ is attributed with saying that when he returns it will be from the east.[8] As Christian prayer is directed to Christ, turning towards the direction of Christ's expected coming is therefore symbolic of turning towards Christ himself. Reference to the dawn is also a metaphorical reference to Christ himself,[9] the light of the world,[10] and thus turning eastwards signifies a turning to Christ (as well as facing towards Jerusalem).

Whatever the origins of the tradition of orientating churches in this way, the effect is that of ensuring that the light of the rising sun shines through the glass of the windows in the east wall. In the early morning, the darkness of the Chapel of the Nine Altars is gloriously transformed. Light refracted by the stained glass produces a dappled abstract pattern of colour on the ceiling high above. Later in the day, as the sun moves higher in the sky, it throws long shafts of light from the clear south window into the lingering darkness of the northern recesses of the Chapel.

The contrasts of light and dark that are thus found here are vividly symbolic of the resurrection of Christ and thus of the resurrection that is the hope of all Christians. As the early-morning light shines onto Cuthbert's tomb, hidden behind the screens of the feretory, it seems almost as though Christ himself, the Rising Sun, might be summoning his servant to rise again and join him in everlasting light. In early afternoon, the sun pouring through the south window can appear to give Fenwick Lawson's huge sculpture of Mary a halo of light. These effects create from time to time a very beautiful atmosphere in this Chapel, which in turn contributes significantly to making it a place symbolic of the hope of resurrection and new life.

Height

The environment that this Chapel provides is shaped significantly by its high vaulted ceiling. Sadly, as it is now approached by almost everyone from the west, along one of the quire aisles, the eye is not drawn immediately to notice this. In fact, the steps down into the Chapel – which lower the floor so as to create a greater sense of height – actually distract the gaze downward when the Chapel is approached, and thus spoil the initial impact of this magnificent effect. If one stands instead just inside the south door, through which it is thought that medieval pilgrims probably entered, the eye is drawn upwards, first towards the beautiful north window, and then higher still to the magnificently high ceiling itself. This sense of height is further emphasized by the numerous slender black pillars of Frosterley marble that decorate the internal buttresses of the east wall between the stained glass windows.

So high is the ceiling of this Chapel that the huge rose window in the apex of its eastern wall is hardly visible at all from ground level. To the extent that the central image of Christ is visible, it seems but a very small image indeed – in contrast to the overruling impression that it creates when viewed from the quire or nave. There is thus an important paradox here: that the elevation that symbolizes transcendence also renders this image of Christ invisible to those who stand closest to it on the floor of the Cathedral. In theological reality also, Christ is both very close to us when we approach him in prayer, and yet so often seems strangely far removed (and may seem furthest away when actually closest). Transcendent and immanent, God somehow can seem at one and the same time, or else at different times, both distant and invisible and yet intimately close at hand.

It is the enormous height of this Chapel that contributes to its majestic sense of the transcendence of God. As the gaze is drawn upwards, it is difficult to avoid a lifting upwards of the thoughts towards a God who is above all things, and in whose presence human beings and human creations (even this Cathedral) seem very small indeed.

Shaping by a Pilgrim Destination

The presence of the feretory has a very practical impact upon the ground floor plan of the Chapel of the Nine Altars. It is this that constricts the Chapel in its middle, so as to make it seem as though it is really two spaces connected by a narrow corridor. Within this corridor almost nothing can be seen of the feretory, but the gaze is drawn upwards and eastwards to the magnificent stained glass that towers above, pointing heavenwards. Thus, the interior of the shrine to Cuthbert, for which this Chapel was built, can not easily be seen from within it, but rather one has to enter one of the quire aisles and ascend the steps which provide access to it before any real impression is gained of what that place is like.

The Chapel of the Nine Altars serves to emphasize the inner sanctity of Cuthbert's tomb on earth, and of transcendent glory above, without drawing undue attention to itself. It offers a representation of the Christian pilgrim, who cannot see his destination clearly, but who presses on in faith, towards his destination hidden in Christ. Reminders of saintly examples of those who have gone before us in following Christ are found here. As they imitated Christ, so we imitate them. Ironically, the living saints – those who walk at floor level with us today – are not always so easily picked out as being holy. Their very ordinariness, their presence alongside us, makes us too easily over-familiar, and even blind, to the presence of Christ within them.

It is this physical shaping of the Chapel of the Nine Altars by the feretory which, I conclude, contributes very significantly to its sense of being a place 'on the way' – a final part of a journey. It is this that marks it out both as an historic place of pilgrimage, but also – in prayer – as a spiritual place of reflecting upon the pilgrimage in which all Christians are engaged, the pilgrimage towards the presence of Christ himself.

Stained Glass

The character of this Chapel is importantly shaped by its extensive and magnificent stained glass. When the sun is shining, this simply offers a blaze of colour, drawing the eye upwards and evoking a sense of divine transcendence and glory. It also offers an overwhelming amount of detail and symbolism, the comprehensive interpretation of which would be a time-consuming task. But within this large glass picture book are some very beautiful and thoughtful stories indeed.

Portraying the life, death and resurrection of Christ, the challenges of Christian discipleship, the lives of Joseph and of John the beloved disciple, and the lives of Saints James, Peter and Paul, these windows offer literally dozens of vignettes of Christian life, in all its vicissitudes. It is as though someone has dipped a huge brush into a pot of paint coloured with all the experiences of Christian life, which has then been splattered onto the canvas of the east and north walls of the Cathedral. But even this image does not do justice to the glorious transmission of light through all these different facets and splashes of colour. The cruci-fixion at the centre of the east wall reminds us that all these experiences are transfused with the light of Christ himself, in whose life, death and resurrection all Christians are called to participate.

At ground level, things are a bit more ordinary. There is colour in the altar frontals, the icon of Hild and the picture of Margaret and David, but it does not transmit light in the same way – it merely reflects it – and at times it is a shadowy and dark place. The visitor to this chapel, especially when sitting next to the feretory and facing east, has to lift his or her eyes upwards in order to fully appreciate the beauty and light that is all around.

Place of Pilgrimage

These four features: illumination from the east, transcendent height, shaping around a destination of pilgrimage, and the colour and symbolism of stained glass, work together to create the peculiar quality, character and texture of this place of prayer. The combinations and permutations of the symbols within this environment must be almost limitless. However, in my own prayers and reflections, the Chapel of the Nine Altars has become primarily a place of pilgrimage – not in the sense of being a destination, for that is located in the feretory, but rather in the sense of being a part of the journey – a place on the way.

All of life is a journey and, for Christians with a divine destination and purpose in mind, it is a journey of pilgrimage. The Chapel of the Nine Altars is a reminder of this context of prayer. Often I have visited it on the journey provided by a single day – perhaps before going to the office or catching a train. Sometimes I have visited it when feeling happy with life, and on other occasions I have brought with me my struggles, sadness and pain. Always it has helped me to reflect upon the divine context in which that day is to be lived. Somehow, I need to lift my head in prayer in order to remember how small I am and how vast creation is, filled with the light of divine glory. I need to be reminded of the lives of saints who have followed Christ before me, and most of all I need to be reminded that my life is a participation in the life, death and resurrection of Christ. I need to remember that my prayers are offered as those of a pilgrim on a journey, a journey towards Christ himself.

In *The Interior Castle*, Teresa of Avila portrays our pilgrimage towards God as a journey through a series of rooms in a castle. God is in the innermost room, deeply within us. The castle is formed of diamond, or crystal, and so is transparent. God, who dwells in the central chamber, shines brightly like a sun, and his light permeates the whole castle. But in the outer rooms this light is only seen dimly. Teresa struggles to explain this. She seems reluctant to suggest that these rooms are actually dark, but nonetheless they are darkened:

> It's as if a person were to enter a place where the sun is shining but be hardly able to open his eyes because of the mud in them.[11]

This metaphorical mud represents all the things that keep us from seeing God clearly: material things, things that we own, our reputation, our work. The closer that we get to that innermost room, however, the more brightly the light of God around us shines.[12] The journey towards God is thus a journey within. As we get to know ourselves better, the more we realize our own need for God to help us in removing the mud from our spiritual eyes:

it is foolish to think that we will enter heaven without entering into ourselves, coming to know ourselves, reflecting on our misery and what we owe God, and begging him often for mercy.[13]

Until we recognize those things within ourselves that prevent us from finding God, we will not find him. But Teresa is also clear that it is only in knowing God that we get to know ourselves.

This returns us to one of the paradoxes with which we began. Prayer is about finding God, but finding God requires prayer. We cannot know God without first knowing ourselves, but true knowledge of ourselves requires knowledge of God.

Untidiness

The northeast and southeast transepts are very different places. The northeast transept is dominated at ground level by the large, proud and elegant marble statue of Van Mildert. The southeast transept is dominated by the equally large, but humble and riven wooden pietà. Around these very different sculptures are a variety of other objects: pieces of decorated stonework, memorials, and a second Fenwick Lawson sculpture partly hidden behind the pietà. These objects have always seemed to me to be somewhat disordered, haphazardly arranged and squeezed in.

This sense of disorder is added to by the asymmetrical structure of the building itself. This reveals itself in the floor level, the stained glass,[14] and even in evidence of miscalculations in the vaulted roof above the southeast transept. Most of this doesn't really matter. After all, beauty is not necessarily ordered, and even divine order is created out of chaos. Cathedrals don't have to be symmetrical, and neither do they have to be altogether tidy. History is not tidy. Perhaps God is not tidy?

In its humility and simplicity, the pietà somehow seems to belong here – even though it is a very new addition to a space that is over 700 years old. It adds to the story told by the stained glass above and behind it, and it brings that story into three dimensions. It speaks of the pain of death. The splits in the wood that run through Mary's face and body are eloquent in their narrative – not only of Mary's pain, but of the pain and wounds in my own life that simply will not go away. I find myself identifying with Mary in her grief. And yet, there is also the polished metal that reflects light and symbolizes life. Into this ordinary, poor, female, human life, made untidy by the intervention of God, is worked divine light and glory.

Lying before Mary is the disfigured and contorted body of Christ. When I look at Mary and empathize with her grief and pain, her hands direct me to look at the crucified body of her son, as though to remind me that my pain and hers are a sharing in his suffering. The sheet metal that is found here is dull and lifeless – although the sculptor reminds us that it is capable of being polished and of reflecting light and life once again. But, most curiously of all, this dead Christ lifts his arm towards his mother as though beckoning us to look back at her and to listen to her story. This is not a tidy, historically ordered, telling of the story of the passion and resurrection of Christ (if indeed any account of such suffering ever could be considered 'tidy'). Life is symbolized here by the raising of an arm that should be dead. It is a reminder that in Christian pilgrimage life and death are all mixed up together. Is this uplifted arm a last gasp of life, or is it the beginning of resurrection? We do not know. Neither possibility is historically or emotionally 'tidy'. The former belongs on the cross, and the latter in the tomb. Neither belong here – at this moment when the body has just been taken down from the cross.

The untidiness of the Easter narrative, as an interruption of our grief, is captured in the last verse of a hymn, written by Rosalind Brown, a Canon at Durham Cathedral:

> You interrupt our mourning, an untrod path you pave;
> for you bring resurrection while we still seek the grave.
> Our lives are wrenched wide open, the wounds we nursed exposed;
> and, like a phrase of music, our death to life transposed.[15]

This 'untidiness', this 'interruption of our mourning', gives us hope. As we share Mary's grief and pain, sometimes it feels as though all our hopes in this world have been dashed and that we do not know what happened to all our dreams. Yet, amidst the driftwood and unpolished metal of this sculpture, there is still hope. In its disorder and darkness it is representative of the untidiness of all our lives, and it offers to help to move our prayers beyond the order of neatly set patterns of words and into the mystery that is God in Christ.

At the north end of the chapel, the beautifully polished statute of Van Mildert is a stark contrast to the pietà. How can it help us in our prayers? Van Mildert, founder of Durham University, like Bede, might be taken to represent the value of learning and the pursuit of truth. But this proud statue doesn't evoke at all the same atmosphere as Bede's tomb in the Galilee Chapel. Its elegance and extravagance speak to the worldly power of the last Prince Bishop. The elevation of the pursuit of knowledge appears here a somewhat presumptuous gesture. Furthermore, this part of the Cathedral has been ordered so that there is nowhere obvious to sit or kneel to pray. It is a place that almost seems to deny prayer. The statue is too tidy, too perfect, too powerful, and lacking in humility.

What can we make of the disorder and untidiness of the northeast and southeast transepts of Durham Cathedral, and their contrast with the proud and tidy marble statue of the last Prince Bishop?

The glass in the Joseph window, behind Van Mildert's statue, reminds us that Joseph was a kind of Prince Bishop too. In Egypt, according to the narrative in the book of Genesis, he became the second-most powerful man in the land, but only after he had been humbled first as a slave and a prisoner. His life was untidy. It reached its divinely ordained destination only after humiliation, suffering, and ignominy. Similarly, Christ was exalted to the right hand of the Father only after he had suffered the shame of the cross. His life was untidy, from conception outside of wedlock to death outside of a city.

The monument to Bishop Van Mildert

It is the light of Christ that guides Christian pilgrimage – or else it is not Christian pilgrimage at all, but only a presumptuous, even arrogant, human gesture. This place of prayer, taken as a whole, reminds us that the darkest and most painful experiences of Christian life are illuminated by the resurrection life of Christ. Sometimes they do still feel very dark indeed while we are still going through them – and I don't know whether the glimmers of light that I see sometimes in these places are the last signs of life before death or the first signs of resurrection. But this is the reality of our participation in the life, death and resurrection of Christ – this is the reality of Christian pilgrimage. It is untidy.

Mothers and Sons

Four[16] different pairs of mothers and sons are presented to us in the Chapel of the Nine Altars.

Mary and Jesus

Fenwick Lawson's pieta portrays Mary, the mother of God, sitting at the side of the body of her crucified son, Jesus. Here, we are confronted with the grief of a mother who held so many hopes for her son – all of which now appear to be dashed. Even the hope that remains (unless we cheat and skip forward to read the story of Easter morning before allowing Mary's story of Good Friday and Easter Saturday to be fully told) is painful and ambiguous. Is this the end of life, or the beginning of resurrection? Either way, nothing can remove from Mary's face the pain of what has happened. When I look at this statue, it is Mary that I am drawn to identify with first. The split in the wood that runs through the statue symbolizes for me the sword that pierced her heart,[17] and it has so often felt as though this sword has pierced my own heart too.

Pietà, by Fenwick Lawson, in the Chapel of the Nine Altars

Margaret and David

Nearby, in Rego's painting, we find another mother and son, also acquainted with grief, but here we are also confronted with deep ambiguity. Margaret and David present a very different scene from Mary and Jesus. Margaret of Scotland (c.1046–93) was wife of Malcolm III of Scotland, and granddaughter of the English King Edmund. Despite her affinity to religious life, she married rather than taking religious orders. She became a reformer of the Church and was known for her charity and prayerfulness. Malcolm and one of her sons died in battle and her other son, David, in turn also became a soldier King.

Rego's portrayal of Margaret is complex. She has her left hand on a gospel book on her lap, suggesting that she cares about God's revelation in scripture. The positioning of her right hand suggests that she cares also for her son. There is a wisdom and a toughness in her face, but the face that looks back at us is not an easy one. It is ambiguous. It could be scheming rather than wise. Then there is the ambiguity of a mother nurturing a child who carries in his hands a weapon of war. What has she taught her son in preparation for his adult life? Wars such as the one that deprived this mother of her husband and son, and this son of his father and brother, cannot always be avoided. Sometimes we need a nurturing that makes us ready to fight, and even more we need a wisdom that is tough enough to know when to fight and when not to fight. But these decisions are not easily made, and often remain open to differing interpretation according to one's point of view. I find it difficult to identify here with either mother or son – I am too unsure about what I make of either of them – and yet they still challenge me about my willingness to make difficult decisions in an ambiguous and hostile world. To abstain from such decisions altogether is to avoid the challenge that Christian discipleship offers.

Mary and John

A little further north, in the stained glass, we see Mary and John standing either side of the crucified Jesus. Unlike the crucifixion scene in the reredos of the Galilee Chapel, only two onlookers have been singled out here. There is no Mary Magdalene holding on to the foot of the cross, no other women are shown as witnesses, and no soldiers stand by. John, or rather the 'disciple whom [Jesus] loved', who is usually taken to be John, is the only male disciple recorded in any of the four canonical gospels as having been present at the crucifixion. This focus on Jesus, Mary and John is evocative of the exchange recorded in John's gospel,[18] where Jesus says to his mother 'Woman, here is your son' and to John 'Here is your mother'. Through these words of Christ, John becomes Mary's son.

As though Mary and John have both immediately been obedient to these words, and have at once taken them to heart, we find another panel, in one of the windows behind the pietà, in which John is to be seen leading Mary away from the cross. The way in which John comforts Mary reminds us that children sometimes have to care for their parents, as well as parents for their children.

These portrayals of Mary and John as mother and son emphasize love and grief. We find that we are present at a crucial point of transformation, for here Mary, the mother of Christ, becomes Mary, mother of the beloved disciple. According to catholic tradition, we see Jesus here affirming Mary as mother of every disciple who loves Jesus, and thus affirming her as mother of the Church. In my reflections upon this scene, I am either there at the cross 'with' Mary and John, or else it is John that I identify with. And so, in this scene, I find that Mary is my mother, and I am her son.

Hild and Caedmon

Further north again, we come to the icon of St Hild. Hild (614–80) was also of royal lineage but chose to enter religious life. In 649 she was made abbess of a religious community in Hartlepool by St Aidan. In 657 she founded the religious community at Whitby, a monastery for both men and women, of which she was Abbess. The community became well known and hosted the famous Synod of Whitby in 664. As far as we know,[19] Hild was not a 'mother' in a physical biological sense, but Bede tells us that she was called 'Mother' by all her acquaintances.[20] She might especially have been considered a kind of mother to Caedmon, whose poetic gift she encouraged and nurtured, or to the sisters and brothers who were members of the community that she founded at Whitby.

I find that I am struck by the powerful influence of Hild's humility and wisdom, and by her nurturing and creativity. In contrast to Rego's portrait of Margaret, there is little ambiguity. Hild was no less realistic about the challenges of politics, but she devoted herself to a life of prayer, and found her enduring influence in or despite her renunciation of worldly power and of opportunities to be a biological mother. There is a balance and harmony about the icon of Hild. It shows her life, from birth to death, as one of charity, wisdom and vision.

Reflections on Relationship

The contrast between Rego's painting of Margaret and Reyntien's icon of Hild is stark. Perhaps this is as much a consequence of artistic style as of theology, history or spirituality. Indeed, perhaps the contrast is emphasized by an awareness of the many things that the two women in reality, in their different periods of history, had in common. But nonetheless, the contrast remains and has influenced my prayers. I want to be like Hild, although in reality I am married with children and seek to serve and follow Christ in a secular world. Perhaps in reality, then, I am more like Margaret? But in the slightly discomforting visage that I find in Rego's painting, as well as in my own experience of life, I recognize that this calling is far from easy. The tension between these two works of art symbolizes for me something of the tension that all Christians experience in combining spiritual devotion and practical care; the tension personified in John's gospel in the story of Mary and Martha.

All of these reflections on mothers and sons, two of which are biblical, two of which are historical (Rego's painting and Reyntien's icon) and one of which (the pietà) is based on speculation about what might have happened – have an Ignatian quality to them. St Ignatius encouraged his disciples to imagine themselves being present in the biblical passages upon which they meditated. Amongst other questions, such meditations present a question as to which character in the passage (if any) the reader identifies with. Here, I have found myself taking a different stance in respect of each mother and son, which is doubtless the result of a variety of psychological, theological and spiritual dynamics. However, I am left especially interested that these mother and son pairs evoke in me different psychological responses according to the understanding of Transactional Analysis (TA).

TA proposes that we operate psychologically in different interpersonal relationships at different times as adult, parent or child. Here, I have found myself as a 'mother' (in identifying with Mary grieving over the loss of the child that is the painless life I would like to have had), an adult (in recognising the challenging reality of the political decisions facing Margaret and Hild) and a child (in finding myself as a child of the Church of Christ). My decision to follow Christ, and thus my belonging to the Church of Christ, necessarily involves me in caring for others, in facing the ambiguous challenges that life presents me with, and in allowing myself to be cared for – by Christ, in and through others.

If we return from this psychological interpretation of what is happening in the Chapel of the Nine Altars to the metaphor of pilgrimage, perhaps we can see here different perspectives upon a single underlying dynamic that all Christians face. Christians are called to take up their crosses and to follow Christ, and thus to participate in the sufferings of Christ. In the process of this we are challenged to make difficult and 'grown up' decisions – recognising that the best of our knowledge is merely ignorance in comparison with the infinite knowledge and wisdom of Christ, and that our bravest efforts pall in comparison with his journey to the cross. We are called to share with others in their suffering, as they make the same journey as us, as though we were mothers and fathers, daughters and sons, to one another, and so to share with Christ in his suffering on his journey to the cross. We are called also to be children, and to receive the comfort that Christ offers us as though we were children and he is our mother – for unless we are able to allow that, we may never reach the destination of our pilgrimage. As Julian of Norwich wrote:

> In our Mother, Christ, we grow and develop; in his mercy he reforms and restores us; through his passion, death, and resurrection he has united us to our being. So does our Mother work in mercy for all his children who respond to him and obey him.[21]

Pilgrim Prayer

In planning a journey, some people are ordered and systematic in researching the shortest or quickest route and in taking a map or directions with them. In some circumstances, they might even make a trial run, to check in advance that they can find their way. Others leave planning to the last minute, ask directions along the way, rely on signs, or take a scenic route. Making a trial run would appear to them a pointless exercise and a waste of time.

The pilgrimage of life is also a journey. None of us can completely plan this journey in advance. Maps and directions tend to be vague, and even contradictory. By and large, trial runs are not permitted, although of course we do sometimes get a chance to learn from our experiences of taking the wrong turning. The Chapel of the Nine Altars provides us with plenty of reminders that life will often be untidy and disordered, littered with wrong turnings and ambiguous signs. Some of us thrive on this, or at least cope with it better than others. Some of us will end up trying to control things that we have no hope of controlling – as though it is possible to plan for every eventuality on a long journey and avoid every delay or detour. Only God knows the journey that we shall take from beginning to end. Only he can control all things, and even then the cross reminds us that he tends not always to use this power in the way that we might hope or expect. But Margaret, Hild and Van Mildert provide us with good Christian examples of planning and using power to good effect for the benefit of the Church and the world.

On a journey, some people prefer to have the map, and others prefer detailed directions which point out landmarks and tell them which turning to take. The maps and directions that we will take with us on life's pilgrimage will include both symbols that need interpretation by map readers and detailed instructions that need to be read carefully. However, it is rare that specific instructions are provided for the decisions presented to us each day, and it is equally rare that the map is always available, or that we know what the symbols on it mean. In the Chapel of the Nine Altars, Van Mildert's statue reminds us of the need to acquire learning and knowledge (detailed instructions) and the icon of Hild reminds us that a complete map of the path of our lives can only be gained when the journey is over.

While some of us enjoy continuing to look at the map rather than choose a path to follow, eventually we all have to make decisions about which way to go. No day allows us to avoid these choices, for in real life failure to take a path is itself a choice to take a particular path. The northeast and southeast transepts of the Chapel of the Nine Altars provide representations of the kinds of processes that are involved in these choices. Thinking – represented by Van Mildert – will always need to be balanced by Feeling – represented by Mary. Decisions based upon rational aspects of being human – planning, understanding and knowing – need to be combined with those based on the emotional aspects that we encounter especially in times of success and failure, loving and losing. Perhaps this is what makes saints like Hild and Margaret special. They were able to bring together these ways of dealing with their world in such a way as to address themselves to both aspects of being human in the world.

Some places become holy because they are a spiritual destination, but all places can become holy when we remember that they are places that we visit on a journey with a spiritual destination. In Christian life, God is that destination, every day takes us further along the journey towards him, and every day provides the opportunity for encounters with him along the way.

It's easy to imagine that the holy places are destinations in themselves and that the journey doesn't matter. However, pilgrimages are journeys that do matter – for their own sake as well as for the destination to which they take us. God reveals himself to us on the journey, amid the untidiness and confusion of life, and in the relationships that we form with one another along the way. If we do not find God on the journey, we might well wonder whether he can be found at all. But praying on a journey is not easy. Journeys are tiring and distracting, and sometimes dangerous, and it will often feel easier to postpone our prayers. Holy places encourage us not to do this.

It seems fitting to close this chapter with a journeying hymn attributed to St Columba (521–97).[22] According to tradition, Columba was exiled from Ireland and became a missionary in Scotland, where he established a monastery at Iona. It was from Iona that St Aidan set out on his mission to the northeast of England.

> Alone with none but thee, my God,
> I journey on my way.
> What need I fear when thou art near,
> O King of night and day?
> More safe am I within thy hand
> than if a host should round me stand.
>
> My life I yield to thy decree,
> and bow to thy control
> in peaceful calm, for from thine arm
> no power can wrest my soul.
> Could earthly omens e'er appal
> a man that heeds the heavenly call?
>
> The child of God can fear no ill,
> his chosen dread no foe;
> we leave our fate with thee, and wait
> thy bidding when to go.
> 'Tis not from chance our comfort springs.
> thou art our trust, O King of kings.

Exploring Pilgrim Prayer

As with the suggestions at the end of previous chapters, the following are offered as prompts only, or perhaps just as a starting point. There are many ways in which the Chapel of the Nine Altars and other places of prayer might be used as places in which to find God.

In the Chapel of the Nine Altars

Spend some time looking at the north window. The story of Joseph is depicted from left to right and from bottom to top, with captions beneath each of the scenes that is portrayed. Although many of these captions are not easily legible, you can read the narrative in the book of Genesis.

The scenes of the window portray the vicissitudes of Joseph's life. We see him lowered into the pit by his brothers, and lifted out of it. We see him thrown into prison and enthroned in power. The sequence begins with a dream and finishes with his death. What have been the pit experiences of your life? What has felt like being in prison or being like a prince (or princess)? What are your dreams? Which panel(s) of the window best illustrate(s) where you feel you are now? Is it a light or a dark panel? How does it feel to be there? Where is God?

Spend some time 'with' the window, and do not rush to bring this to an end. However, when sufficient time seems to have elapsed, and when it feels right to do so, remind yourself of where you are and be aware of the presence of God with you in the here and now. Use the following prayer (another verse from St Patrick's breastplate) or another prayer to ask God to be with you in whatever circumstances you face in your life at the present time.

> I bind unto myself today
> The power of God to hold and lead,
> His eye to watch, His might to stay,
> His ear to hearken to my need.
> The wisdom of my God to teach,
> His hand to guide, His shield to ward;
> The word of God to give me speech,
> His heavenly host to be my guard.[23]

In the Chapel of the Nine Altars or Another Cathedral or Church

When you arrive at the east end of the north or south quire aisle of the Cathedral, or at the east end of an aisle of the church or chapel that you have chosen, pause for a few moments and look around you. Which place do you find most attractive as a place in which you might spend some time in prayer? Spend some time there praying quietly. Be aware that God is with you there.

If you were on a journey through this cathedral, church or chapel, which place within it might best represent the place you feel you have reached in the journey that is your life? Spend some time quietly in this place. How does it make you feel? What things around you come to your attention, and what do they represent to you at this stage in your life? Be aware that God is with you there.

Which place within your surroundings might best represent the place that you would like to be in life? Move to that place, or at least direct your attention more closely to it. Spend some time reflecting upon it and upon what it might mean to you. Be aware that God is with you there.

Before you leave, move again to the place in which you first started. Be aware again that God is with you there, as he has been in all of the places here in which you have prayed, and as he will be in all of the places to which life will take you in the future. Ask before you leave that you might become more aware of his presence with you in all that lies outside this cathedral, church or chapel, and that he will guide you to the places that you will visit in life's journey where you will meet with him.

Blessed those who find their strength in you, whose hearts are set on pilgrimage[24]

In Another Place

Plan and undertake your own pilgrimage to a holy place. This need not be expensive, time consuming or exotic. In fact, it might be better to plan a 'pilgrimage' on the way to work, which might only last half an hour, rather than to go on a trip halfway around the world – especially if the latter becomes a busy holiday rather than a time for prayer. Your pilgrimage could be anything from a small detour during a working day to a planned visit to a holy place. The important thing is that you are visiting a special place for a spiritual purpose, as an expression and act of prayer.

There are many ways to choose the best place to visit for this pilgrimage. It might be a place that represents something significant for you on your life's journey – a place to which you have been, in which you find yourself, or to which you would like to go. It might be a recognized 'place of pilgrimage' – such as Holy Island in the northeast of England or Assisi in Italy – or it might be a place that is special to you alone. It might be a church, shrine or retreat centre, or it might not be a religious place at all. It might be a place with literal and physical symbolism – a cross, altar or work of art – or it might be somewhere that symbolizes something special to you in a much less explicit and visible way. For example, it might be a place that you visited at an important point in your life, or a place which you have always wanted to visit, or simply a place in which you have found peace.

You might like to pray as you set off on your journey – giving expression to the particular purposes for which you are making this visit. However, remember that the journey itself is your prayer and that you are travelling to find the reasons for making it as much as you are making it for any conscious purpose of which you might be aware. Do not be too self-conscious along the way. Enjoy the journey, simply noticing the sights and sounds and smells and other things that come to your attention. God is present in these things and is not only to be found when you reach your destination.

When you reach your planned destination spend some time in quietness and listen to what God might be saying to you in this place. Allow the things that you see and hear and smell to assist you in your prayers, but be open also to the things that cannot be physically seen, heard or sensed in other ways in this place. What words best express what you find here? What words best express what you would like to say to God in this place? Don't worry if you can't express these things in words – that is why you have made this journey. Simply be aware that you are here as an expression of your desire to find God – here and in every place.

Before you leave you may like to light a candle, make the sign of the cross, or leave something as a token of your visit.

As you journey back again – to home or work or everyday life – remember that you are still travelling *towards* God. The real pilgrimage is to find God in every part of every day and in every place.

> My dearest Lord
> be Thou a bright flame before me
> be Thou a guiding star above me
> be Thou a smooth path beneath me
> be Thou a kindly shepherd behind me
> today and for evermore. Amen.[25]

Chapter 7

Contemplative Prayer: The Feretory

Durham Cathedral was built as a place of prayer: a place for pilgrims to come to for prayer and a place in which a monastic community would pray. Its situation on the Durham peninsula, and its character as a holy place, were determined from the outset by the presence in this great church of the earthly remains of St Cuthbert, a saint noted for his life of holiness and prayer. His burial behind the high altar, at the eastern end of the Cathedral, provides the spiritual focal point of the Cathedral.

The influence of St Cuthbert upon this place is enduring, even a millennium after it was built. But what exactly is that influence, and what might it mean to those who visit his tomb with time to reflect and pray today? And what kind of prayer might the feretory, within which St Cuthbert is buried, suggest or encourage?

First, let us turn to look briefly at what we know about Cuthbert, and about the history of this place and those who have prayed here. We will then turn to consider the influence that all of this might have upon those who pray thoughtfully and reflectively in this place today.

St Cuthbert

Cuthbert was born in c.636 CE. According to St Bede, Cuthbert entered the monastery at Melrose while still of such an age as to be called a 'boy'. In 664 he became Prior of Melrose, and subsequently he became Prior of Lindisfarne, but it seems that at some point he developed a longing for a solitary life of prayer and became a hermit on the small island of Inner Farne. In 685 he reluctantly consented to be ordained bishop of Lindisfarne. Bede tells us that:

> As bishop he followed the example of the blessed Apostles and enhanced his dignity by his holy actions, protecting the people entrusted to him by his constant prayer and inspiring them to heavenly things by his salutary teachings. Like a good teacher, he taught others to do only what he first practised himself. Above

all else, he was afire with heavenly love, unassumingly patient, devoted to unceasing prayer, and kindly to all who came to him for comfort. He regarded as equivalent to prayer the labour of helping the weaker brethren with advice, remembering that he who said, '*Thou shalt love the Lord thy God*', also said '*Love thy neighbour*'. His self-discipline and fasting were exceptional, and through the grace of contrition he was always intent on the things of heaven. Lastly, whenever he offered the sacrifice of the Saving Victim to God, he offered his prayers to God not in a loud voice but with tears welling up from the depths of his heart.[1]

Some months before his death on 20 March 687 he withdrew again to Inner Farne, and it was here that he wished to be buried. St Bede, recording the words of Herefrith (another monk who became Abbot of Lindisfarne), quoted Cuthbert as saying to his monks:

it is my desire to rest here where I have fought my fight for the Lord and where I want to finish the course and whence I hope to be raised up by my just judge to receive the crown of righteousness. What is more, it would be less trouble for you if I did stay here, because of the influx of fugitives and every other kind of malefactor which will otherwise result. They will flee for refuge to my body, for, whatever I might be, my fame as a servant of God has been noised abroad. You will be constrained to intercede very often with the powers of this world on behalf of such men. The presence of my remains will prove extremely irksome.[2]

Eventually, however, in response to the pleading of his monks, Cuthbert is recorded as saying:

If you feel you must go against my plans and take me back [to Lindisfarne], I think it would be best to make a tomb in the interior of the basilica – then you will be able to visit it yourselves whenever you wish and also to decide who else from outside may do so.[3]

Cuthbert's body was thus brought back to the monastery at Lindisfarne for burial there. Eleven years after his death, his coffin was raised so that it could be entombed above ground – an act that reveals the esteem in which he was already held at that time. When this was done, however, his body was found to be incorrupt:

On opening the coffin they found the body completely intact, looking as though still alive, and the joints of the limbs still flexible. It seemed not dead but sleeping. The vestments, all of them, were not merely unfaded but crisp and fresh like new, and wonderfully bright.[4]

This sign was treated as further and miraculous evidence of Cuthbert's holiness.

Subsequently, the dangers imposed by Viking raids necessitated the abandonment of the monastery on Lindisfarne. By 875 all of the monks had been killed and the community of St Cuthbert left Lindisfarne.

The Feretory, showing the tester above St Cuthbert's tomb

For seven years, carrying with them Cuthbert's body in his coffin, they travelled to places given to Cuthbert and then for 113 years they settled at Chester-le-Street, just north of Durham. In 995 they finally settled in Durham. The body was eventually translated to the present Cathedral, which was specifically built to house it, in 1104.

St Bede wrote his *Life of Cuthbert* in about 721. It abounds in stories of miracles associated with Cuthbert's intercessions, sometimes showing similarities with biblical miracles, which are recorded as having taken place both during his life and after his death. However, it is not just the miraculous with which Bede wanted his subject's memory to be associated:

> So full was [Cuthbert] of sorrow for sin, so much aflame with heavenly yearnings, that he would never finish mass without shedding tears. He would imitate, as was only fitting, the rite he was performing, by offering himself up to God with a contrite heart. He urged his people to lift up their hearts and give thanks to the Lord God more by the yearnings of his own heart than by the sound of his voice, more by sighs than by chanting. His thirst for righteousness made him quick to reprove wrong-doers, but his gentleness made him speedy to forgive penitents. Often as they were pouring out their sins he would be the first to burst into tears, tears of sympathy with their weakness, and, though he had no need, would show them how to make up for their sins by doing the penance himself. He wore quite ordinary clothes, neither remarkably neat nor noticeably slovenly . . .. By these and other similar spiritual works the venerable prior fired all good men with the desire to emulate him, and recalled the wicked and the rebels against the rule from their obstinacy in error.[5]

Even allowing for the elaboration and exaggeration of Bede's medieval account, it is hard to read the *Life of Cuthbert* and not be left with the impression that this was the story of a man who showed compassion to those in his pastoral care, who sought to follow Jesus Christ, and who loved nothing better than to know the presence of Christ in the sacraments and in prayer.

Medieval Pilgrims' Prayers

St Cuthbert's shrine came to be one of the most important destinations for pilgrimage in medieval Europe. That importance was reflected both in the strength of faith that ordinary Christians had in the power of St Cuthbert's prayers and also in the lavishness of the decoration of the shrine itself. In the *Rites of Durham* it is recorded that the shrine provided four places for pilgrims to kneel:

> in time of their devout offerings and fervent prayers to God and holy St Cuthbert, for his miraculous relief and succour which being never wanting made the shrine to be so richly invested, that it was estimated to be one of the most sumptuous monuments in all England, so great were the offerings and jewels that were bestowed upon it, and no less the miracles that were done by it.[6]

On certain festival days, the cover of the shrine would be raised, an event to which pilgrims and other Cathedral visitors would be alerted by the sound of bells attached to one of the ropes from which it was suspended:

> the bells did make such a good sound that it did stir all the people's hearts that were within the Church to repair unto it and to make their prayers to God and holy St Cuthbert.[7]

The coffin itself was gilded, with pictures on the east end of Christ sitting on a rainbow in judgement and on the west end of Mary with the Christ child on her knee. Within the shrine, or feretory, were recesses within which were kept holy relics and gifts offered by pilgrims. In the rear of the Neville screen, which was then colourfully decorated, were alabaster statues, also highly decorated.[8]

The impression created by the feretory must have been breathtaking. Presumably it would have been at least partially visible to pilgrims as they entered the Chapel of the Nine Altars, from which it was then separated by an iron railing surmounted by candles. Then as now, pilgrims would have ascended the steps to the north or south of the feretory to gain a closer view. Finding themselves at last within the intimate confines of this space, in close proximity to the earthly remains of St Cuthbert, at the spiritual heart of this enormous cathedral, they would have offered their prayers.

Such prayers would usually have been offered at the end of long and sometimes dangerous journeys, and often with particular needs in mind. One can imagine that intercessions for the health and safety of the pilgrims themselves and their friends and family would often have been at the forefront of their minds as they knelt to pray. But presumably motives for making such journeys were many and diverse, as in the case of Chaucer's Canterbury pilgrims. If a pilgrimage is a journey made with a spiritual purpose, it nonetheless appears that human beings are often able to deceive themselves as to what their true purposes of heart and mind really are. There is every reason to believe that this was no less true in the Middle Ages than it is now. An expressed desire for piety can more or less successfully conceal an interior motivation of pride. An expressed concern about the health of another might easily have provided a publicly acceptable reason for making a journey that was really a quest for personal forgiveness, atonement and peace. Perhaps for some there was a superstitious expectation that visiting this place would make all things right. But the woman who, according to Mark the Evangelist, touched the hem of Jesus' garment might easily have been condemned as superstitious too.[9] And this place, surely, also provided – then as now – a space in which pilgrims could reflect upon what they feared, or knew only too well, was in their own hearts.

Whatever the reasons for setting out on such a hazardous undertaking, the feretory represented the glorious earthly destination of these pilgrims and thus also, metaphorically, their hope of attaining the spiritual purpose for which they had set out on their journeys in the first place. But the medieval splendour of the feretory contrasted deeply with the simplicity, asceticism, and humility of the saint whose body it contained.

The Reformation and After

At the time of the Reformation in England, the monastery at Durham was suppressed and Durham Cathedral was stripped of much of its wealth and decoration. Statues of saints were removed from the Neville screen and elsewhere in the Cathedral. Forty-nine niches on the east side of this screen alone, the side facing the feretory, remain empty today. The shrine of Cuthbert was dismantled and taken away, along with its relics, gold, silver and precious stones. In time, the colourful decoration of the Neville screen was also completely removed and it was returned to bare stone.

Elsewhere in England, as for example at the shrine of St Thomas in Canterbury, the bones of saints were removed from their resting places and were burned. In Durham, however, when the tomb was opened, it is recorded that the body of St Cuthbert was again unexpectedly found to be still intact. The body was eventually re-interred beneath the site of the original shrine. Cuthbert's earthly remains are therefore today still buried below a simple black marble slab bearing the name 'CVTHBERTVS'.

Ironically, then, the unexpected discovery of the preservation of Cuthbert's body on different occasions half a millennium apart had parallel but contrasting outcomes. The first, on Holy Island, led to elevation of the body above ground, to veneration by Catholics and later to a pilgrimage around the north of England that culminated in Cuthbert's tomb in Durham becoming itself a destination of pilgrimage. The second, in Durham Cathedral, inadvertently initiated by Protestants, led to the reburial of Cuthbert's body below ground in an effort to prevent its veneration. But, contrary to Protestant intentions, it thus remained there for the benefit of future pilgrims, who continue to visit it to this day.

The Reformation transformed the shrine of St Cuthbert. This transformation revealed itself in terms of what was then considered 'politically correct', as well as in its more tangible impact on what the feretory looked like. Pilgrimage, which had largely been publicly viewed as a worthy venture, was increasingly viewed with the keen suspicion that the Reformers brought to bear upon all traditions that were not obviously (to them) supported by scripture. An appreciation of representations of the saints as reminders of Christian belonging to the communion of saints was replaced with suspicion of idolatry.

Cuthbert's shrine was thus transformed from something that was rich and splendid to something that was and is profoundly simple. The Reformation undid the wishes of the monks who sought to venerate Cuthbert's holiness by elevating his coffin above ground level. It did nothing to return Cuthbert's body to the place in which he would most like to have been buried, on the Inner Farne. But it did introduce to the feretory an element of simplicity that is more consistent with what we know of Cuthbert's life than was the worldly wealth and splendour that preceded it.

In the twentieth century, colour returned to the feretory in the form of two banners that hang on the columns to the north and south of Cuthbert's tomb, and a tester that hangs over the tomb itself.

The banners were painted by Thetis Blacker, and the batik work employed in their creation made use of the remains of candles that had been lit in the Cathedral by visitors who had come to pray. The northern banner portrays St Oswald, sword in hand, mounted on his warhorse. (The association of Oswald with Cuthbert derives both from the seemingly strange decision to bury Oswald's head in Cuthbert's tomb,[10] but also from the association of both saints with St Aidan, who founded the monastery on Lindisfarne and who brought Christianity to northeast England.) The southern banner portrays St Cuthbert, dressed as a Bishop of the seventh century, and accompanied by some of the creatures that he would have known well on Lindisfarne and Inner Farne.

Above Cuthbert's tomb, the tester – a kind of canopy – portrays Christ in glory, after the visions of the books of Ezekiel and Revelation.[11] It was designed by Sir Ninian Comper, and was hung in the feretory in 1949.

The tomb itself, the focus of this sacred space, remains a simple black stone slab.

The Feretory as a Place of Prayer

When medieval pilgrims entered the Cathedral through the south door in the Chapel of the Nine Altars, the elevated exterior of the feretory would have been one of the first sights to confront them. Perhaps through gaps in the railings surrounding it, these pilgrims would have caught a first tantalising glimpse of the treasures within. Today, it is usually encountered only after a walk from the west end of the Cathedral, and then only after descending and ascending flights of steps on the north or south side. It is thus the intimate, and now relatively simple, interior of the feretory which first confronts the pilgrim or tourist who ventures deeply within the Cathedral itself.

But gaps and openings in the screens that surround the feretory prevent this from being a completely enclosed space. To the east the great expanse of stained glass in the Chapel of the Nine Altars is visible. To the west, glimpses of the sanctuary, quire and tower are visible through the Neville screen. Above, the tester provides only a very partial ceiling, and the tapering stonework of the Neville screen points to the ceiling vaults high above. This is therefore an enclosed space that exists in explicit and visible relationship to the Cathedral within which it is situated. It is intimate and defined, yet also open and permeable in its boundaries.

I think that this physical character of the feretory is very important – for it says something about the nature of all prayer. Firstly, we have to make the effort to find this place. It is in itself a destination that takes us off the beaten track of our daily lives. It requires a mini-pilgrimage to reach it. But then, when we have taken the detour, we find ourselves in a very paradoxical place. On the one hand, we withdraw deeply within to the intimacy of communion with a God who alone knows our deepest thoughts, but on the other hand we find that in prayer we catch glimpses of all that is going on in the Cathedral around us, and our spiritual eyes are diverted to the beauty and transcendence of all that lies above and beyond us. So we are at the same time alone with God in our hearts, but also deeply aware of all that lies around us. Prayer is not a place of hiding from the world, but rather a place of engagement with it.

Of course, I am assuming here that we find ourselves alone with God in this place. For most visitors, however, this is not their experience. The feretory is usually a place in which we encounter others who come and go both as pilgrims and tourists. The world outside the Cathedral is not visible from within the feretory, but rather it comes and goes in the human form of those who visit it. Today's visitors are very different from those who came as medieval pilgrims. Many, perhaps most, appear largely curious, albeit perhaps also appreciative of what they see. Few visitors stop to pray; although it is still the case that people's motives for visiting this place are only visible to God and not to other human beings. Most people observe the signs that urge quietness and seem caught up, more or less, in their own thoughts.

Prayer, like the feretory, is a very paradoxical place, in which our inner world, and the world around us, and the world of Cuthbert, and the Kingdom of Christ, are all strangely mixed together. It is a place of permeable boundaries. It is a place of encountering the transcendent, that which is infinitely beyond our confinement in time and space, but also of immanent encounter with that which is intimate, deeply within and close at hand. It is a juxtaposition of that which denies God with that which acknowledges his presence. It is an approximation or engagement of thoughts and desires and hopes and aspirations that cannot be seen with visible realities that form the material world around us.

I think that it is this paradoxical nature of the feretory, brought about by history, architecture, and human cognizance of the holy, which most contributes to making it such a special place in which to pray. However, it is also a special place in which to pray for a number of other reasons. Amongst these, is its unusualness as a Christian Chapel in not having a cross at its focus – either on the tomb itself, or on the small altar that stands between it and the Neville screen. Furthermore, the positioning of pews and a prayer stall to the eastern side of the tomb, and the creation of a path which allows visitors to walk around the eastern side of the tomb on their way from south to north, or north to south, results in a reversal of the usual orientation of a Christian church towards the east. In this space, anyone who stops to look or pray tends to find himself facing west – towards the tomb in the floor and the Neville screen behind it.

There are lots of potential distractions from the focus that Cuthbert's tomb provides within the feretory. There are the banners and the tester, not to mention a headless statue, thought to be of Cuthbert himself, carrying Oswald's head in its left hand. The beautiful stained glass of the Chapel of the Nine Altars is easily visible through the wooden screen that surrounds the eastern half of the feretory. Above are the vaults of the early Gothic roof and away to the west glimpses can be caught of the quire and tower. But this space has a very clear focus within, in the form of the tomb itself, and the obvious place in which to sit and contemplate this focus is on its eastern side, so that the Neville screen falls behind it.

The Neville screen, even bereft as it is today of its medieval colour and alabaster statues, is a very beautiful thing indeed. It is graceful and delicate. Its pinnacles point heavenward, but it is firmly rooted in the ground of this world. Behind it lies the high altar – the Eucharistic point of focus of the Cathedral. The spaces where the larger statues used to stand now form windows into the quire, although these windows are too high to reveal anything much below half the height of the interior of the Cathedral. There is no cross on this screen, but there are the 49 small recesses on its eastern side, within which statues of the saints once stood. There is also, suspended from an iron bracket, a sanctuary candle, which burns here continually. The screen has two doors, one to the north and one to the south, which are usually locked shut.

As I have sat and prayed in this place, wondering what it all says to me about life and about my place in this world, and my relation to God, it has seemed significant that it is a screen that I see when I lift my eyes from the tomb.

Death is of course the screen that denies all living people sight of that which lies beyond. As Christians, we believe that we have caught glimpses of what lies beyond that screen. Supremely we find these glimpses in the New Testament accounts of the resurrection of Christ, which are the foundational basis of all Christian hope. We find glimpses also in the lives of the saints: both those who have died before us, and also those living saints whom we encounter in this world today. We find glimpses also in the Old Testament – such as in the apocalyptic account of the book of Daniel, portrayed in the tester that hangs above Cuthbert's tomb. But still we see all these things only as glimpses. The closest we get to anything clearer and greater is in Christ himself, and even then we find that this clear view is conveyed to us somewhat indirectly – through the gospel accounts, through the sacraments, and through the lives of his followers.

The material world around us is also a screen. On the one hand, it is rich and beautiful, glorious, breathtaking, life-sustaining, fascinating and mysterious. On the other hand, it is cruel, painful, chaotic, decaying and dark. Whether we are caught up in the richness of its beauty, or in the poverty of its suffering, we are always distracted by its visibility and tangibility. It is so easy to imagine that it is only what we can see with our eyes, and touch with our hands, and hear with our ears that is real: that is really there at all. Christ challenges us to think again. In caring for the poor, and in sharing their poverty, he denies our insistence that only material wealth matters. In suffering crucifixion he denies the myth that comfort in this world is all that matters. In rising again he affirms that there is life beyond what we can see, and touch and hear and taste and smell in this world. Cuthbert, in his asceticism and self-denial for Christ, in his prayerful willingness to follow Christ, in his concern for ordinary people, affirmed what he saw in Christ as being of greater value than what he saw in the material world around him. Behind the screen of what is tangible in this world lies a different order of values, and Cuthbert calls us to join him in affirming its priorities.

But a screen is not only something that conceals. It may have doorways and openings, through which light is transmitted, through which we may catch glimpses of something beyond. As already mentioned, we catch such glimpses in scripture, in other human beings, and in the sacraments. But we also catch glimpses of divine glory in a creation that everywhere reflects the beauty and glory of its creator. A screen is also something onto which an image can be projected, and the screen of creation seems to have the image of God projected onto it. At times, this beauty can seem so great that it is more as though this screen becomes transparent and transmits images of God to us, rather than that it merely reflects images of God projected onto it. And even in the midst of human pain and suffering, which can at times seem so unbearable, there are the gospel accounts of God's presence in the midst of all that is dark and insufferable. It is as though at times, perhaps the very best and worst of times, but also some of the most ordinary times, the screen evaporates and we are left in direct contact with the Divine.

I think that it is not merely the symbolic, perhaps even the sacramental, significance of finding a screen in the feretory that makes it a special place but, because it is a screened-off place, at the heart of which lay the earthly remains of a follower of Christ who is separated from us only by the screen of death, it invites us to stop and reflect and pray in the midst of our own lives. What matters to us? What do we see when we look around us – in the feretory or in the world outside? What were Cuthbert and the saints remembered and even venerated for? Will others look back on our lives when we move to the other side of the screen and recall that they met Christ in us, or will our lives reflect other priorities to them? In the quiet space that the feretory provides, we are given a screened-off place in which to ask such questions and search for answers.

The Banners of St Cuthbert and St Oswald

If the feretory speaks to us of the importance of reflecting on the reality that lies behind visible things, the banners of St Cuthbert and St Oswald which hang within it offer us differing images of how lives may be lived in accordance with those realities.

To the north, the banner of St Oswald presents an image of courage, determination and allegiance to truth. It is an image that challenges all that is counter to the Kingdom of Christ, but which does so in a very politically realistic way. The sword held in his right hand, inscribed with the words 'Pro Pace' ('For Peace'), makes clear what it is that Oswald stands for, but also leaves us in no doubt that he is willing to fight for it. In case there was still any doubt, however, there is behind him the cross of Heavenfield, the place at which he defeated the pagan King Cadwallon and won Northumbria for Christendom.

Oswald's banner includes a dove of peace, as well as a Raven symbolic of war, a pool symbolic of healing, and bread symbolic both of the Eucharist and of charity to the poor. In her commentary on the banner, the artist has indicated that it is intended to show that 'through sacrifice and suffering of war come eventual reconciliation, peace and healing'.[12] But this banner also reminds us that sometimes following Christ requires us to fight for what we believe in. It is a challenging image, not just because Oswald died in battle (which reminds us of the potential cost of fighting for what we believe in) but also because Christ himself so clearly eschewed the use of physical force as a means of bringing in his Kingdom. This is not to say that just war theory is entirely without merit, or that there is never a place for literally fighting for what we believe to be right. It is rather a reminder of the agony that is the lot of those who struggle with decisions about whether or not to engage in direct confrontation with that which they believe to be wrong. For all that such confrontation must sometimes be necessary in this world, Christians can never forget that they follow one who chose not to take up arms.

To the south, St Cuthbert is portrayed as Bishop of Lindisfarne, servant of Christ and of the Church of Christ in this world. He is making the sign of blessing with his right hand, as though to bless all who enter this holy place. The creatures surrounding him provide reminders of at least two of the miracles found in Bede's *Life of Cuthbert*, but they serve also to remind us of the natural environment within which Cuthbert loved to pray. The overall effect of the banner is to emphasize the spirituality and holiness of Cuthbert, but it does not allow us to forget (if we know anything about Cuthbert's life) that this holiness did not shirk the very real sacrifices associated with the service of Christ in this world. Cuthbert did not hide away in prayer, but rather engaged in a life of service in a context of prayer.

Not that we should imagine that for Cuthbert prayer was a life of peaceful solitude and recollection. Rather, he viewed prayer as a form of warfare against the forces of evil. In this, the challenge of the two banners becomes apparent. Oswald won his battle at Heavenfield, against human odds, after erecting a cross in front of his army and calling his soldiers to pray with him. Cuthbert won his battles in prayer on Inner Farne in the context of belonging to a praying community at Lindisfarne. Prayer is the Christian calling. For Oswald this calling entailed a willingness to fight, having prayed. For Cuthbert it entailed a willingness to fight in prayer. For Oswald, it was a political and practical matter of winning and ruling an earthly Kingdom. For Cuthbert, it was a spiritual and pastoral matter of caring for Christ's Church. Christian vocations are not all the same, but neither are they completely different from one another. We are all called to a life of prayerfully following Christ, along with all the challenges to our wisdom, love and courage that this will present.

> Lord God almighty,
> who so kindled the faith of King Oswald with your Spirit
> that he set up the sign of the cross in his kingdom
> and turned his people to the light of Christ:
> grant that we, being fired by the same Spirit,
> may always bear our cross before the world
> and be found faithful servants of the gospel;
> through Jesus Christ our Lord.
> Amen.[13]

The Tomb and the Tester

Above Cuthbert's tomb hangs the tester with its colourful portrayal of Christ in glory. At the corners are four creatures, each with two wings, traditionally used to symbolize the four evangelists, together with the names of these evangelists in Greek.[14] Either side of Christ is portrayed a six-winged creature, a seraph.[15] From behind Christ, and radiating all around him, are three-dimensional rays of gold, which catch the Cathedral lighting in such a way that they almost appear to emit light themselves.[16] On the edges of the tester are inscribed references to the annunciation, the names of the apostles and the archangels Michael and Gabriel, and the orders of heavenly beings.[17] This imagery echoes the iconography of Cuthbert's original coffin, which bore images of Christ and the four creatures on its lid, images of apostles and angelic beings on its respective sides, and images of the annunciation and the archangels Michael and Gabriel at its respective ends.

The tester is highly colourful, with a gold background and the central figure of Christ portrayed largely in blue and red. The contrast with the simple black stone below, with its inscription, could hardly be more marked. The tester is glorious, splendid, and full of light. The tomb is cold and dark, simple and stark.

The symbolism of the tester is apocalyptic, drawing upon texts from Ezekiel and Revelation:

> In front of the throne was a sea as transparent as crystal. In the middle of the throne and around it, were four living creatures all studded with eyes, in front and behind. The first living creature was like a lion, the second like a bull, the third living creature had a human face, and the fourth living creature was like a flying eagle. Each of the four living creatures had six wings and was studded with eyes all the way round as well as inside; and day and night they never stopped singing: Holy, Holy, Holy is the Lord God, the Almighty; who was, and is and is to come.[18]

Its texts include reference to heavenly figures, principally to various orders of angels, as well as to Mary, the four evangelists, and the 12 apostles. The inclusion here of the latter, along with the empty niches in the Neville screen, provides a reminder that those who are Christ's followers in this world will share in his resurrection and thus in eternal life with him. It is, crucially, the gospel accounts of the life, death and resurrection of Christ which provide Christians with the hopeful basis for this participatory link between the visible, tangible, reality in which we live, and the unseen but greater heavenly reality which is hidden from us as though behind a screen.

Visitors at ground level find themselves closer to Cuthbert's tomb than to the tester. Cuthbert provides another reason for hoping in all that the tester tantalisingly promises. As he followed Christ, so we are invited to follow Christ and so to join with the whole communion of saints – in this visible world and in the heavenly reality that is hidden from our sight – in rejoicing together in his life, love and glory. But our closeness to Cuthbert's tomb prevents us from escaping into dreams of a heavenly reality that are merely escapist. Our proximity to the simplicity, balance, darkness and tangibility of this slab of marble remind us that participation in the life of Christ in this world is not always glorious, comfortable or attractive. Christ calls us to take up our cross and follow him, and this is at times a very dark place indeed in which to be with him. If we are to participate with him in his resurrection, then we must first be prepared to participate with him in his passion.

The darkness of the tomb also reminds us that there is an apophatic, as well as a cataphatic, tradition in Christian spirituality. While the latter rejoices in all that can be said about God, and especially in all that can be said about God in Christ, the former recognizes that the gulf between an infinite Creator and finite creatures is so great that all that we can know or say about divine reality will be as darkness in comparison with the light of divine glory. The *Cloud of Unknowing* provides one of the classic expositions of this theme.[19] All that we know about God must fall short of the reality – for that reality will always be infinitely greater than mere finite creatures can grasp – and so, eventually, knowing God will paradoxically require an unknowing and a letting go of all that is less than God.

The apophatic tradition is concerned not only with unknowing but also with contemplation of God out of a deep desire and love for him for his own sake. It is only such a love that will be prepared to share with Christ in his suffering in this world, or which will find him present amidst all that is most painful, hopeless and dark. It is this love, it seems to me, that Cuthbert symbolizes for us here in this place. And even if Cuthbert's love for Christ was somewhat exaggerated by Bede, we are left with the very real expression of that love which Bede himself conveyed in his writings – for it was clearly something that he and Cuthbert shared.

Perhaps this is why I often find myself praying here not only the collect for St Cuthbert, displayed on the prayer stall in the feretory, but also the prayer of St Bede, which is displayed on the prayer stall in front of his tomb in the Galilee Chapel, with its reference to drinking in 'with delight the words of [God's] knowledge' and its expression of desire to stand one day, forever, before God.[20] While words are delightful, and convey knowledge of Christ, ultimately all that the contemplative wants to do is to be *with* Christ. This, it seems to me, is what both Bede and Cuthbert wanted more than anything, and it is in this that we are called to follow them.

The juxtaposition of the tester and the tomb are another reminder that there is an unseen reality behind all that is visible. This is portrayed firstly in a vertical axis (above/below) rather than the horizontal (in front/behind) one of the Neville screen. Secondly, it is portrayed in a temporal axis ('already but not yet'). But the apophatic and cataphatic traditions ultimately take us to a place in which all physical metaphors break down completely. There is only one reality. It is firmly located in Christ. Equally firmly it is beyond all imagining. It is exemplified in the life of Cuthbert, but it finds its location in the hearts of all who love Christ from the deepest depths of their own desiring.

Contemplation of Christ in Space and Time

The feretory is a place with strong associations with a particular follower of Christ – St Cuthbert. These associations, its history and architecture, all lend to it a particular spiritual and psychological atmosphere, which is complex, subtle and multiform. I say it is multiform, for I am quite sure that there will be both similarities and also many differences in the thoughts that it evokes for me and for its other visitors. I know that I am not alone in finding it a very special place. This specialness has undoubtedly contributed to my motivation in writing about it. But ultimately, it is not the specialness of the place about which I am writing at all. It is the uniqueness of God in Christ. It is the Christian reality that exists both within and beyond time and space.

In writing about this place, I find that I am also writing about myself, or at least about the story of the Christian Church, a story in which I participate. I have come to this place with my own troubles, joys, concerns and experiences of life, just as many others have before me. I have come to pray when I have been afraid, downcast, tired, uncertain, lonely, in company, expectant, inspired, joyful, or at peace. I have come as pilgrim and as tourist and as a member of the local church community. I have come with things to say, and I have come in silence. I have come to ask Cuthbert for his prayers. I have come most of all, however, just to be with Christ.

Amidst these varying moods of life, I have found within the feretory a peaceful sense of the presence of Christ. I have found comfort in being a part of the communion of saints. I have found a place within which to collect my thoughts and prayers. The banners have come to symbolize for me the tension between my own desire simply to be alone with Christ in prayer and the recognition that Christ also calls me to service in the world and in his Church. The tester reminds me of the hope that I have of one day seeing Christ in glory. The simple black slab of stone, however, challenges me more than all of these things.

The darkness of the stone, upon which I find the name of one of Christ's followers, reminds me of the darkness of sharing in his sufferings. It reminds me that Christ calls me to take up my cross and follow him. Knowing the fellowship of Christ, and of Cuthbert, in my sufferings does help. But suffering still hurts. The darkness also reminds me of the unknowing that I still need to do. My best vision of Christ in glory, symbolized here by the tester, will be empty darkness in comparison with the true reality. The simplicity of the tomb reminds me finally that Christ is not to be found in richness and power, or amidst great fanfares, but in poverty and in silence. And I think that that is perhaps why I am most pleased to come. For here I sense the presence and love of Christ, the one and only thing that is truly needful.

Contemplative Prayer

Contemplative prayer appeals more to some people than to others and can take different forms for different people. The reflections that I have offered in this book find their seeds in the world of sensory perception and only then make connections with the symbolism and abstraction of intuitive thinking. For some people this will provide an easy way in to contemplative prayer. For others it will be unnecessary or even unhelpful. Most of us find contemplation hard at times, for it takes us not only beyond the world of sensory perception, of facts and data, but even beyond our deepest imagining. It is the prayer of unknowing, of going beyond sensing and intuition.

Again, contemplative prayer is the prayer of being, and of perceiving, rather than of doing. But we must not forget that 'perceiving' in this context goes beyond perceiving in the usual sense. Perceiving God is an unperceiving, as much as it is an unknowing. God can be perceived in all things, but is also hidden by all things. If perceiving God is pure prayer, then it is a prayer that takes us beyond human limits.

BUT now you will ask me, 'How am I to think of God himself, and what is he?' and I cannot answer you except to say 'I do not know!' For with this question you have brought me into the same darkness, the same cloud of unknowing where I want you to be! For though we through the grace of God can know fully about all other matters, and think about them – yes, even the very works of God himself – yet of God himself can no man think. Therefore I will leave on one side everything I can think, and choose for my love that thing which I cannot think! Why? Because he may well be loved, but not thought. By love he can be caught and held, but by thinking never. Therefore, though it may be good sometimes to think particularly about God's kindness and worth, and though it may be enlightening too, and a part of contemplation, yet in the work now before us it must be put down and covered with a cloud of forgetting. And you are to step over it resolutely and eagerly, with a devout and kindling love, and try to penetrate that darkness above you. Strike that thick cloud of unknowing with the sharp dart of longing love, and on no account whatever think of giving up.[21]

I have suggested that there might be a vocabulary of holy places in order to facilitate a process of thinking about what exactly it is that holy places say to us. But if holy places invite us to pray, and if prayer is about finding God, we will ultimately find ourselves lost for words. Whilst Christians will always use words in prayer, words will never be enough. According to Bede, Cuthbert was aware that love of neighbour was also 'equivalent to prayer'. But his desire to withdraw to the remoteness of the Inner Farne suggests that he understood that other ways of prayer were also needful. I do not think that he withdrew there only to say the same prayers that he would have used on Lindisfarne. Surely, it was the silence of this place, its stillness, its wordlessness, that he sought?

Contemplative prayer can be challenging and bewildering. It is sometimes easier to retreat to the safety of words, of things that we can see and hear and taste and smell and touch. Sometimes, contemplative prayer will be facilitated by such things and it is not necessarily the case that we must eschew all perceptions or all speech in order to pursue this kind of prayer. Contemplative prayer is not an obsession with avoiding the material world or our humanity. But it is a being with God that goes beyond all these things and it leads us into a kind of silence that is at times frightening and frustrating, as well as deeply attractive and alluring. It is here that we find God in prayer, and it is to this intangible holy place that visible, geographical, holy places beckon to lead us.

≈≈◉◉≈≈

Exploring Contemplative Prayer

The feretory presents us with contrasting images of prayer: colour and darkness, activity and stillness, words and silence. These contrasting approaches to prayer can be explored in many different ways. A few suggestions are offered here as to how contemplative prayer might be explored in the Feretory or elsewhere.

In the Feretory
Spend some time in the Feretory looking at the two banners and reflecting on them.

What do each of the two banners symbolize in your life? In what ways do you find yourself following Oswald in actively serving, or even fighting for, Christ? In what ways do you find yourself wanting to withdraw from activity in order to pray or simply be with Christ? Which of the two banners do you most identify with? Which best represents your life as it is, and which best represents your life as you would like it to be? (You may wish to spend some time at home or elsewhere in using some art materials to create banners which represent your own actual or ideal life as a follower of Christ.) If there is a tension for you between the actual and the ideal, to what extent is this creative and to what extent does it suggest that things need to change?

Before you leave the feretory, kneel at the stall in front of Cuthbert's tomb, and pray the collect that is used in Durham Cathedral services for St Cuthbert's day:

> Loving Father
> whom the whole company of saints adore:
> we rejoice with all our hearts in Cuthbert,
> glory of our sanctuary
> and ever-living example of our apostleship.
> Help us to follow his example
> by the simplicity of our lives
> and by the power of our witness;
> through Jesus Christ our Lord. Amen.

In the Feretory of Durham Cathedral or in Another Cathedral or Church

Durham Cathedral is not alone in having a screen from which statues have been removed. Some churches with niches still have statues of the saints, and almost every church or chapel has its tombstones. Find a screen or tomb or wall that appeals to you in some way. Spend some time sitting or kneeling in front of it in prayer. In your prayers, you may want to reflect upon what the screen or tomb conceals? What do you project upon it? What do you enjoy or appreciate about this place? What frightens or unsettles you?

If there are associations of this place with particular saints, find out what you can about who these men or women were and reflect upon the different ways in which they followed Christ. What example have they left? In what ways can they encourage you as you seek to follow Christ?

To finish your time of prayer, you may like to pray the Prayer Book collect for St Cuthbert's day:

> Almighty God
> who didst call thy servant Cuthbert from keeping sheep
> to follow thy Son and to be a shepherd of thy people;
> mercifully grant that we,
> following his example and caring for those who are lost,
> may bring them home to thy fold,
> through thy Son Jesus Christ our Lord.
> Amen.[22]

Cuthbert left his work as a shepherd of sheep[23] to be a shepherd of Christ's human flock. What does he call you to leave, and what does he call you to take up?

In Another Place

Find a place in which you can be alone to pray in contemplative silence. This might be amidst the isolation and anonymity of a crowded place or else in a remote and secluded place, but try to find a place in which you are unlikely to be disturbed. Ensure that you will have at least a few hours to spend there. If this cannot be on one day, then it might be possible to spend a half an hour or so in that place on each of a series of days. Alternatively, it may be helpful to plan a retreat or holiday on which you can have more time for your prayer. However, if you are able to do this, don't try to spend longer than an hour or so at a time in focused prayer, unless this comes naturally or easily to you. About an hour at a time is usually best in terms of concentration.

If you are able to go on retreat, it may be possible to ask a Retreat Centre if they can provide a director or guide for you, who will be able to offer individual and more detailed advice on how best to use your time in prayer. Periods of silence and isolation can allow all kinds of things to come into our minds, which can be puzzling, disconcerting or challenging in a variety of ways. If you don't have a retreat director to speak to, it would be a good idea to find a good spiritual director with whom you can discuss your experiences in prayer. It may also be helpful to keep a journal in which you can record your experiences.

Periods of silence and unstructured prayer can be exciting, stimulating and enjoyable – but they can also be difficult, unsettling or challenging. Sometimes they can be rich and present an abundance of material for reflection, and sometimes they can seem arid and desert-like. Patience, wisdom and courage are all important qualities for such prayer, and can be nurtured by such prayer.

Cuthbert saw his time on Inner Farne as battle with the demons, as well as meeting with God. What are the 'demons' with which you are faced when you are alone in prayer? In what ways does God meet with you in such times? You may like to pray the verse of St Patrick's breastplate in which the 'Christ's incarnation' is invoked:

> Against the demon snares of sin,
> the vice that gives temptation force,
> the natural lusts that war within,
> the hostile men that mar my course;
> of few or many, far or nigh,
> in every place, and in all hours
> against their fierce hostility,
> I bind to me these holy powers.[24]

Chapter 8

Holy Places: Finding Ourselves and Finding God

My hope in recording the personal reflections that have formed the basis for this book is that they will encourage others to go and do their own reflecting and praying and to explore their own holy places in a way that will be relevant and illuminating for them. Each person who visits Durham Cathedral, or any other holy place, brings to it their own unique personality, their own unique history, their own inner places of hurt, hope and encounter with God. Visitors to holy places may come looking for God, or they may not. They may encounter God, or they may not. But they may also find out important things about themselves and, sometimes, it may be in the process of the encounter with oneself that God is found.

Holy Places

Durham Cathedral is, and long has been, recognized as a holy place far beyond the borders of County Durham, and is admired by those of all faiths and none.

Nathaniel Hawthorne, the nineteenth-century American novelist, wrote in *The English Notebooks* of his visit to Durham in 1857:

> We paused upon the bridge, and admired and wondered at the beauty and glory of this scene, with those vast, ancient towers arising out of the green shade, and looking as if they were based upon it. The situation of Durham Cathedral is certainly a noble one . . . Grand, venerable, and sweet, all at once; and I never saw so lovely and magnificent a scene, nor (being content with this) do I care to see a better.[1]

The contemporary American travel writer Bill Bryson,[2] has more recently and famously given Durham Cathedral his vote for 'best

143

cathedral on planet Earth' and in 2001, listeners to BBC Radio 4's *Today* programme voted it as Britain's favourite building.[3]

In this book I have sought to identify and reflect upon what it might be that evokes these responses and, more particularly, what it is that evokes my own responses to this place.

There is, of course, the beautiful, groundbreaking and awe-inspiring architecture that defines this holy place and which so uniquely questions and challenges the person who encounters it. Similarly, the dramatic location of the building, and the relationship of its various parts to each other, have influenced a number of these reflections. Perhaps these physical considerations, defining as they do the visible and tangible nature and location of this holy place, tap into some kind of unconscious or archetypal structures within the human psyche.

Then there is also the consideration that this has been a place of prayer and of celebration of the sacraments for more than nine centuries. Here have been offered the prayers of men and women, asylum seekers, prisoners, miners, students, pilgrims, penitents, monks, priests, lay Christians and people from other faith traditions or from no particular faith tradition at all, all of which have hallowed and permeated the spiritual atmosphere of the building. I find huge encouragement in knowing that countless people have prayed in this place before me and that, together, we are all a part of the communion of saints – in heaven and on earth: for this I am very grateful.

In addition to the physical structure of the place on the one hand and its spiritual history on the other there are further factors that contribute to the special quality that draws pilgrims and others to this place and on which I have been reflecting here. There are the dedication of the Cathedral to Christ, Blessed Mary the Virgin and St Cuthbert, the various purposes to which this place has been put over the centuries, and the orderings and reordering of it with which they have been associated. There are the beautiful objects and features within it that symbolize and communicate aspects of the relationship between God and human beings. All of these things work together to have a particular effect that is conducive to prayer.

I have suggested also that there is a vocabulary of holy places, comprising words which somehow communicate holiness. Pilgrims to holy places seem to understand instinctively what these words mean, even if they aren't consciously aware of it, and even if different individuals interpret them (according to their personality and life story) in different ways. This vocabulary includes words such as darkness and light, pilgrimage, scale, silence, symbol, timelessness and even untidiness.

These words point us to something beyond yet also close at hand, something holy. They draw us into a relationship, or a conversation, that is prayer. In the end, however, we are exploring something that is ineffable and which defies all of the words and images that we have explored in this book. Where the metaphor ends, we are left with Rudolf Otto's assertion that the 'numinous' is simply something that we perceive instinctively, like a sixth sense.

Finding Ourselves in Holy Places

Each person will bring to a holy place their own preferences for finding life, relating, perceiving, deciding and praying. Some will prefer to kneel alone, in silence, and others will prefer to find themselves a part of a large congregation. Some will notice details, and others will see symbols and metaphors that point to something beyond. Some will be caught up in feelings evoked within, and others will be drawn to explore the history and affairs of the building around them. Some will simply want to be still and take it all in. Others will be drawn into making decisions about the implications of it all for their own lives, and their understandings of God and the world.

Even individuals with similar personality will each come with their own different experiences of life and of prayer and of other holy places. As a result, each will bring their own unique and hidden inner places into the common surroundings of this vast and very visible holy place. These hidden inner places will either resonate with or interfere with the environment provided by this outer holy place. Previous encounters with the numinous might be reawakened; or perhaps visitors still mentally and metaphorically take hold of the knocker on the north door, hoping that they will find refuge here from the accusations that life presses upon them. Perhaps also some find that the encounter of their inner places with this holy place is too painful. I wonder how many visitors react against this holy place, defending themselves against the claims that they fear it might make upon them?

Durham Cathedral, and other holy places like it, resonate with things that lie beneath the level of consciousness within the human psyche. Doubtless they do this in different ways for each of us, but their beauty and their darkness echo things within us that we have either forgotten or else have never fully appreciated. These things may be the best and worst parts of ourselves, and they may be things that are associated with strong emotion. Perhaps, in Jungian terminology, they are archetypal themes that underpin what it means to be a human being – a spiritual being – in this material world. We may ignore these themes, and choose not to interpret them, but holy places offer us an opportunity to explore our own inner selves as well as our faith, our human society and our common humanity.

Throughout this book, I have explored the theme of place. Usually, this has been a literal reference to holy places in the world around us – notably Durham Cathedral, but also to places such as Inner Farne, which was so special to Cuthbert, and the innumerable and often very ordinary places in which readers of this book will have made their own encounter with the Holy. I have also referred to place in a metaphorical sense: the places within our hearts and our lives in which we have encountered the Holy. In both cases, it seems to me that holy places are a kind of text in which we may read about God and his saints and their encounters with one another in years gone by. We read something about where we have come from, about the meaning and purpose of our own lives here on earth today, and the destination in Christ towards which we are headed. Praying in a holy place is therefore an exercise in interpreting this text: in theological terminology, a hermeneutical exercise. What conclusions we reach as a result of this exercise will depend upon the hermeneutical tools that we use: our theology, our historical-critical awareness, our use of allegory and, not least, our own personal responses to this text, the echoes that it finds in our own hearts and minds. For this reason, it will reveal as much about each of us as it does about God in Christ and the Church. For this reason, it will mean many things to many people, as well as revealing some central truths which may be found in it by almost everyone.

When we walk into a place such as Durham Cathedral we are incorporated into its story, even if only for a short time, and we are interpreted by it, just as we seek to interpret it for ourselves. Of course, this will only happen if we stop to think: to ponder what it all means, and what we might mean within it. In much the same way, some people will read a good novel and will find within it only an exciting story. Others, stopping to reflect upon it, find themselves within its pages – each in their own unique way – and so their lives are the more greatly and uniquely enriched by their reading.

If this is the case, then how has Durham Cathedral interpreted me? I have mentioned some of the things that I have found as I have written each of the chapters of this book. Most obviously, I have found myself interpreted as being but a small part of something much greater, a small part of creation and eternity and of God's mission in this world. I have found myself in the Chapel of the Nine Altars, and in the feretory, challenged about my willingness to be both prayerfully and actively engaged in Christ's service, following the examples of Hild, Margaret, Oswald and Cuthbert. I have found myself at the sculpture of the Annunciation in the Galilee Chapel being asked whether I am willing to say 'yes' as Mary said 'yes' to God, and then at the pietà in the Chapel of the Nine Altars wondering whether I can still hope in God's salvation even when, like her, all my dreams seem to be shattered. But, perhaps most of all, this holy place has comforted, challenged and drawn me over the question of whether and where I find God within myself, amidst my struggles, my pain, my hopes and my dreams.

Finding God in Holy Places

Prayer can of course be offered anywhere at all and perhaps the deepest and most profound prayers have been offered far away from holy places. Prayer can be offered in the midst of physical or psychological pain, in the face of social exclusion or discrimination, in drab or dispiriting surroundings, and even in response to the unholiness of deliberate human cruelty or the denial of all that is good and beautiful. It is certainly not necessary to come to Durham Cathedral, or any other holy place, to pray and there would be something dreadfully wrong if prayers were only offered in such places. Nevertheless, holy places are a kind of sacred space in which our prayers are facilitated in some important psychological and spiritual ways. It is as though they allow our lives, our joys, our hopes and fears, our pain and struggles all to become mixed up with those of the saints who have gone before us, and most importantly of all with those of Christ himself. And perhaps visiting and praying in such places thus becomes one way in which we can grow in prayer and begin to explore our lives in such a way that everywhere becomes a holy place.

I suggested in Chapter 1 that 'finding God' is what prayer is all about. This book has been about the process of engaging in prayer, in this search for God, in holy places, and especially in one holy place, Durham Cathedral. The reader might legitimately ask at the end of the book, has God been found?

I hope that the reader who has persevered thus far will have seen that there is a deep and multi-layered paradox in the whole notion of 'finding God in a holy place'. It has been said to me, for example, that it would have been more interesting, surprising or challenging to write about finding God in an unholy place. But then, if God were to be found in such a place, surely it too would be holy – not unholy?

And one of the things that emerges from acquaintance with Durham Cathedral is that it does in any case have its dark, unholy, side. Its history and fabric betray a human fear of sexuality masquerading as the displeasure of God and St Cuthbert, a lust for power which pretended to serve, and a pride that exalted itself above others in the name of the Church. It has been a prison as well as a church, a place of exclusion as well as a place of invitation. Exploration of this holy place leads us to some pretty unholy places. In a sense, it is an unholy place as well as a holy one. But I don't think that the Christian explorer should expect that it could have been otherwise, for God seems to turn up in unholy and 'God forsaken' places like Gethsemane and Calvary.

In any case, the whole notion of finding God, wherever he may be found, is paradoxical. The author of *The Cloud of Unknowing* reminds us that if we want to know God we have got to do a lot of unknowing. Similarly, I think that if we want to find God, we have got to have lots of experiences of not finding him, or even of losing him. There are, for example, all the inadequate, shallow and false ideas of God that we have accumulated as a result of our capacity to settle for the comfortable rather than uncomfortable, the safe rather than the challenging, the convenient rather than the inconvenient, and the understandable rather than the confusing. These need somehow to be lost before we can find God as he truly is. There is also the major problem surrounding our own finitude. If God is infinite, and is everywhere, we do not need to find him. Perhaps it is rather that we need to allow ourselves to be found by him? And in any case, if we do find him, we will never be able to take in the infinite magnitude of what we have found.

Is the whole search pointless, then? I don't think so. I think, rather, that the search is infinitely rewarding. If God is everywhere, then he can always be found, even if only in the process of struggling with the experience of seeming not to have found him. But this already reminds us that we do have to be clear that we want to find God, and not merely want to feel as though we have found him.

I have suggested that, in Durham Cathedral, there is something in the nature of the place that helps us in our search. The nave, the quire, the Galilee Chapel, the Chapel of the Nine Altars, and the feretory, each offer their own clues and encouragements to us in our search. I think that other holy places are similar. In Northumberland, for example, different parts of Holy Island each offer their own aids to prayer. These aids to prayer are not very different to those explored in this book in relation to Durham Cathedral. There is the intimacy of the Boiler House Chapel at the St Cuthbert's Centre, and the wild,

Holy Island

'marginal', remoteness of the sand dunes. There is the rhythm of daily prayer at St Mary's Church, and the encouragement to pilgrim prayer of the causeway. All of these could have been written about in similar terms to those used here in respect of Durham Cathedral.

What I think is interesting, is that each of these 'aids to prayer', these different aspects of holy places, if we respond to their invitation, take us beyond the place itself. The nave of Durham Cathedral does not only invite us to pray when we are sitting in it, it beckons us to be involved in the life and mission of the Church and to pray outside its walls. The quire invites us to pray every day – not only when we are able to sit in its stalls at Morning or Evening Prayer. The Galilee Chapel, especially, reminds us that we will only really find ourselves in a holy place when we step outside, when we go beyond the margins of what is defined (by some) as holy. The Chapel of the Nine Altars challenges us to see the whole of life as pilgrimage towards God. And the feretory challenges us to be contemplative in our prayer, to know God in unknowing, and to find God in losing him.

God can be found in holy places. But when we find him in such a place, we discover that he is everywhere. Not least, we find him deep within ourselves. If God is deep within each of us, then what we mean by 'finding' God is actually not the discovery of the Divine presence at the end of a journey from a place where he was not to a place where he is. Rather, we mean that we *feel* his presence, or have *become aware* of it, or have begun to *understand* it in some small way. The journey is therefore within – from an inner place of not feeling, not being aware, and not understanding to one of feeling, awareness and understanding.

Since beginning the process of writing this book, I have begun to think about other times and places in which I have felt something of the same sense of the divine presence that pervades Durham Cathedral. In the middle of a big city, in a shopping centre, in a library, in other cathedrals, on the holy island of Lindisfarne, at the Franciscan Friary at Alnmouth, in spiritual direction, in cafés, and even in my own home, amongst other places, I have been aware of something of the same sense of the presence of God, in different ways and to varying degrees. Usually, this has been peaceful, encouraging, reassuring, hopeful and beautiful – as for instance sitting on Holy Island and being aware of God's presence in the beauty of land, sea and sky, in the sparkling of light on water, in the birds circling overhead and in the reminders of prayers offered there over many centuries.

However, sometimes the sense (feeling, awareness, understanding, etc.) of the presence of God has been challenging, discomforting, painful, dark and forbidding and has even been a sense of absence as much as of presence. The pietà in the Chapel of the Nine Altars and the painting of the Crucifixion in the Galilee Chapel especially remind me of prayers offered on dark nights of struggling at times in my own life when God has seemed absent and evil has seemed to have the upper hand. There is thus another layer of paradox. On some of the occasions when I have not felt, or been aware of, or understood God's presence I have in fact found him. An inner journey from a place of feeling, being aware and understanding to one of not feeling, not being aware and not understanding can also sometimes be a process of finding God.

It's hard to discern whether it is my struggling with prayer in these other times and places that has made prayer in Durham Cathedral all the more meaningful, or whether it is actually the other way around. But I know that prayer in this holy place has somehow helped me to pray in other places: places in which it has sometimes seemed more difficult to find God. These include the places within my own life that have sometimes felt God forsaken and unholy, as well as the more mundane and ordinary places in the world around me in which God is not so obviously present.

I can't help but identify the same experience in Bede's account of the life of Cuthbert, and especially in his account of Cuthbert's desire to spend time on his beloved Inner Farne. On visiting Inner Farne today it is easy to see how Cuthbert found God here amidst the beauty, isolation and wilderness of this place. For him it was a place of struggling with demons, as well as a place of encounter with God. But it seems to have been his encounters with God in this holy place – as well as on Lindisfarne and in other holy places – that enabled him for a wider life of prayer and service as a monk, a priest and a bishop in Christ's Church.

I am thus brought back to the paradox with which I started this book. God is to be found everywhere around us and within. And yet, he seems to be present more in some places and at some times than others. Exploring these times and places with a view to finding God in them seems to help us to find God at other times and in other places too, so that eventually we discover that he is in fact everywhere. The process of exploration will be different for each of us, but the one God whom we search for expresses himself in diverse ways. Thus I have found God through different people, as well as in different places: people like Cuthbert, who lived long ago; people whom I have met only through their writings, like Bede; and others who are alive today. In varying ways and to a varying degree they share that sense of holiness that pervades Durham Cathedral, but even more so, for in them it is incarnate in human form: in them it is the presence of the living Christ in his body, the Church.

But, of course, I am only one person who has prayed in this holy place, and there are many people in the world, and not a few holy places. Perhaps this book is therefore really a reflection upon finding God in the many and in the one, for God is the One that pervades the many. In the diversity that exists within and between holy places and holy people, God is somehow found in many ways, and yet always proves to be the same. If there were no diversity, no differences or distinctions between places and people, not only would the world be a poorer place, but I think it would in fact be harder to find God in it – even though he would still be omnipresent. The seeming absence of God in some places, and his seeming presence in others, somehow points us in the right direction, so that we can, eventually, find him everywhere.

Not all of us progress along this pathway of discovery at the same rate or in the same way. Thus some people continue not to find God anywhere, while others find him everywhere, and most of us find God in some places and either fail to notice him, or else fail to find him despite all our efforts, in others. At a service in Durham Cathedral, the Bishop of Jarrow once observed that 'If you can't find God here, you aren't trying!' Of course, he and I both know that the atheist won't be convinced (although doubtless there will always be some people in some places who find God even when they are not trying, or perhaps even when they are trying not to find him). But, for the person who is trying, there will always be places in which God can be found. Amongst these places are some in which most of us can find God most of the time – even if we aren't trying very hard. Durham Cathedral is one of those places.

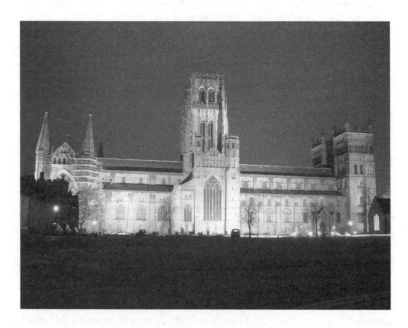

Durham Cathedral at night, from Palace Green

Notes

Chapter 1: Finding a Holy Place: Durham Cathedral

1 Mt. 27.45, Mk 15.33, Lk. 23.44
2 Mt. 27.33, Mk 15.22, Lk 23.33, Jn 19.17
3 Church of England, 2005, p. 499
4 Davies, O'Loughlin and Mackey, 1999, pp. 300–301
5 Iconography of angels was found on St Cuthbert's coffin, and the ninefold order of angels is listed on the side of the tester over his tomb in Durham Cathedral (see Chapter 7).
6 Church of England, 2005, p. 40. This prayer was written by St Anselm. Another of his prayers may be found in Chapter 5.
7 50–75 mm of sandstone was removed from the exterior in order to improve the weathered appearance. Alas, many of the original Norman features have thus been lost. A reminder, perhaps, that the way things appear here now may not be the same as it was in the past.
8 The knocker which is presently to be found on the north door is a replica. The original may be seen in the Cathedral treasury.
9 Unfortunately, the Chapter House and Prior's Hall are not normally open to the public.
10 The name of Cuthbert was removed from the dedication at the time of the Reformation, but was recently restored.
11 http://www.durhamcathedral.co.uk/introduction
12 Rice, 1994, p. 120
13 Sadgrove, 2006
14 Ibid., p. 8
15 See, for example, Pritchard, 2002 or Duncan, 2000.
16 For example, you may like to read Silf, 2004, McGreal, 1999, or de Waal, 1984 respectively.
17 Jer. 29.11–14a

Chapter 2: Finding God in a Holy Place

1 2 Chron. 6.18
2 Acts 17.28; This quote of St Paul is itself a quotation from an unknown classical philosopher.
3 Ps. 139.7–12
4 Mk 6.3
5 Mk 15.34
6 Gen. 28.11

7   Gen. 28.16–17
8   Otto, 1980
9   Exod. 3.5
10   Exod. 3.6
11   The story may be found in Mk 9.2–8, Lk. 9.28–36, Mt 17.1–8
12   Space prevents a detailed coverage of this important topic here, but the interested reader is directed to Bruce Duncan's excellent book *Pray Your Way* (Duncan, 2000).
13   Lk. 10.41–42
14   Munitiz and Endean, 1996, p. 329

Chapter 3: An Invitation to Pray: The Nave and the Body of the Church
1   Rev. 4.4
2   I am grateful to Lilian Groves for her permission to quote this story.
3   For example, these columns, if they could be opened out, would be squares with four equal sides, variously understood to represent the four evangelists, the world, or even the Divinity.
4   Wolters, 1966, p.68
5   In the central apex of the window, is a lamb (representing Christ). To the right and left of this, in the apices above the scenes of the annunciation and the visit of the Magi respectively, are a dove (representing the Holy Spirit) and a sun emanating three rays of divine light (representing in this case God the Father as the un-begotten source of the Trinity).
6   Jn 1.5
7   The moveable 'Benedict' platform allows the situation of an altar at the east end of the nave, in front of the screen that separates the nave from the quire. When this platform is not in use, the high altar is visible at the east end of the sanctuary, in front of the Neville screen. However, although this altar is not located in the nave itself, it still very clearly provides the point of focus at the east end of the Cathedral at ground level, just as the rose window provides a higher point of focus visible above the altar in the east wall.
8   C. F. Alexander's translation of this hymn, published in 1896, may be found in many hymn books, but the reader may also like to refer to David Adam's meditations on the hymn of St Patrick (Adam, 2000).
9   Jn 1.14
10   Rev. 4.8b
11   Rev. 4.11
12   Ibid.
13   Jn 1.12–13
14   Jn 6.32, 33, 35, 56
15   Mt. 25.31–46
16   I do recognize that the Eucharist is not a feature of life in the Salvation Army. This statement is not intended to be exclusive of Christians who do not share my sacramental theology. However, it is my understanding that Salvationists would understand their participation in Christ in non-sacramental ways, no less important to them.
17   Tobin, 1991, p. 179
18   Mk 10.38–40
19   vv. 21 & 32

20 Further reflections on the life of St Cuthbert are offered in Chapter 7.
21 Further reflections on the life of St Bede are offered in Chapter 5.
22 Jn 10.14–15
23 Church of England, 2005, p. 487
24 Jn 1.1–5

Chapter 4: Daily Prayer: The Quire and Sanctuary
1 Fry, Baker, Horner, Raabe and Sheridan, 1982
2 See, for example, Mk 9.30–37.
3 For example, '*Laudate dominum in tympano et choro*' and '*Laudate dominum in chordis et organo*' would appear to be references to Ps. 150.4.
4 See, for example, Miller, 1995, p. 49. However, it appears that this is not exactly what Augustine actually said. The often attributed quotation seems rather to be a paraphrase of a part of Augustine's commentary on Ps. 72.1: 'he that singeth praise, not only praiseth, but only praiseth with gladness: he that singeth praise, not only singeth, but also loveth him of whom he singeth. In praise, there is the speaking forth of one confessing; in singing, the affection of one loving.' (This translation taken from the Christian Classics Ethereal Library CD, v4, Calvin College, Grand Rapids).
5 Sadgrove, 2007, pp. 112–115
6 Stanwood, 1967, p. 111
7 *Book of Common Prayer*, p. 658
8 Or at least, almost in full! In Durham Cathedral various verses, and even an entire psalm, are omitted. Various reasons are put forward for this, and a full examination of the merits and demerits of this practice would be too big a diversion here. Perhaps it will be sufficient to say that some of the anger against evil expressed by the Psalmists presents a challenge to Christians who are called to love their enemies. If these verses are interpreted as an expression of anger against all that sets itself against God, including that within the human psyche, as the present author would prefer, they can be helpful indeed as expressions of prayer. The danger, however, is that they are interpreted too literally as self-righteousness and a bloodthirsty desire for God to hurt other human beings who have hurt us.
9 Church of England, 2005, for example, on p. 115.
10 Denoted in *Common Worship* by a small red diamond (here a small black diamond) at the end of a line, to show where the break occurs.
11 Ibid., p. 729
12 Ibid., p. 676. cf Mk 15.34
13 Ibid., p. 678
14 Ibid., pp. 117–8
15 Ps. 150.1
16 '*Laudemus viros gloriosus*', on the north side, appears to be from the Latin Vulgate translation of Sir. 44.1 which can be translated in English (from the Latin) as 'Let us now praise men of renown and our fathers in their generation'. '*Homines pulchritudinis studium habentes*', on the south side, appears to be a partial quotation from 44.6 which (in full) can be translated in English as 'Rich men in virtue, studying beautifulness: living at peace in their houses'. It would seem to me that the location of these texts invites us to look at the whole of this hymn of praise as applicable to St Cuthbert, whose shrine lies only a few metres away, on the other side of the Neville screen.

17 Ps. 68.19
18 Ps. 1.1–3
19 There are various pocket editions of such prayer books which might be helpful if you want to use this basis for prayer when travelling. See, for example, Stancliffe, 2003, Warner, 2004, Society of Saint Francis, 1996.
20 Church of England, 2000, p. 168

Chapter 5: Praying on the Margins: The Galilee Chapel

1 Mk 1.14b
2 25 metres by 15 metres.
3 The stone of these columns has been eroded, probably as a result of the use by nineteenth-century university students of coke braziers for heating. Purbeck 'marble' is in fact a form of limestone obtained from Dorset, and was brought to the northeast of England by sea.
4 The present windows in the north and south apparently date from the fourteenth century, and in the west wall from the fifteenth century. The overall sense of lightness may thus have been enhanced. However, mouldings in the stonework high above the inner south aisle suggest that clerestory windows were perhaps considered and deemed unnecessary, presumably because the Chapel was already provided with sufficient light by its original windows.
5 William White, addressing the Royal Institute of British Architects in 1890, argued that this was its initial primary function and that no altar was dedicated within this space until the fifteenth century.
6 Translation by Dr Diana Barclay.
7 See Marner, 2000.
8 In addition to strengthening the interior columns (so that each pillar now comprises four columns rather than only two), Langley added external buttresses and re-roofed the chapel.
9 Interestingly, the door was opened once more in 1845, but the vista was thought to be disappointing. The door was closed and the Langley altar replaced.
10 Although there is a north door which is occasionally used to provide an access to the main cathedral via the Galilee Chapel.
11 It has been suggested that this was, in fact, a part of the process of encouraging female pilgrims to come to Durham.
12 Sherley-Price and Latham, 1988, p. 33
13 Browne, 2002, pp. 12, 45, 57, 60, 92
14 This cross, in the alcove on the east wall of the inner north aisle, and the text from Bede's commentary on Revelation, mounted on similar wood and taking a similar position in the inner south aisle, were introduced to the Galilee Chapel during the 1970s.
15 The statue is dated 1981. Interestingly, the Pyrz statue (not in Durham) entitled simply 'Annunciation' is dated 1984. As the latter includes an angel announcing God's message to Mary, while the Galilee statue shows her pregnant, the latter is presumably numbered 'II' for reasons of the chronology of the story that it depicts, rather than because of the chronology of its creation.
16 The triptych (attributed to Van Orley, c.1500) which now hangs over Langley's altar was donated to the Cathedral in 1935.
17 Lk. 1.26–38
18 By Josef Pyrz (b.1946).

Notes 157

19 Mt. 20.22–23, 26.39; Mk 10.38–39, 14.36; Lk. 22.42, Jn 18.11. A similar observation has been made in relation to Rublev's famous icon of the Trinity, where the three figures seated around the table also outline the shape of a chalice.
20 It is Mary Magdalene, for example, who is consistently shown in tears.
21 Lk. 2.35
22 Although there is still a medieval portrayal of the crucifixion high on the south wall of the inner north aisle.
23 The higher wall paintings on the south wall of this aisle, and the images of Cuthbert and Oswald on either side of the altar are, of course, much more clearly visible. However, sitting in a pew at the back of the aisle and facing east these images are not easily visible.
24 Ward, 1973, pp. 202–3
25 Ward, 2003, p.132
26 Mt. 4.12–16
27 Jn 19.25–30
28 Slee, 2004, p. 18. © Nicola Slee. Used with permission.

Chapter 6: Pilgrim Prayer: The Chapel of the Nine Altars
 1 From Fowler, 1903, p. 3 (with rendition into contemporary English by the author).
 2 Four scenes from their lives are depicted, each illustrating a text from the King James Bible. From top to bottom, these represent: Mt. 14.30, Jn 21.17, Acts 9.4 (cf 22.7, 26.14), Acts 26.27. Above each of the main sections within this window is an angel holding a text. Together, the texts form a quotation from Ps. 118.1 ('Give thanks unto the Lord; for he is good: because his mercy endureth forever').
 3 These include John reclining next to Jesus at the last supper (Jn 13.23), John leading the grieving mother of Jesus away from the empty cross, John finding the empty tomb with Peter (Jn 20.3–6), Peter and John healing the man lame from birth at the Gate Beautiful (Acts 3.1–10), and John's vision in Revelation of the Lamb enthroned in heaven (Revelations 4 & 5). The designer of the window would clearly have assumed that the John who wrote the book of Revelation was the same John who was author of the fourth gospel. Quite apart from the fact that this was never necessarily the case, and that the Bible itself does not give any reason to suppose that the authors of these two books were one and the same John, the authorship of the fourth gospel is any case disputed. The 'beloved disciple' referred to in the fourth gospel may or may not be the author of that gospel.
 4 The building of the Solomonic temple, the child Jesus debating with the doctors of the Law in the second Jerusalem Temple, and St John in the heavenly Jerusalem.
 5 In the north window is the birth of Jesus (Lk. 2.7), the flight into Egypt (Mt 2:13–14), and the baptism of Jesus (Mt 3.13–17, Mk 1.9–11, Luke 3.21–22). In the central window is a scene showing Jesus carrying his cross (Jn 19.17) with a much larger portrayal above of the crucifixion itself, with Mary and John standing on either side of the cross (Jn 19.25–27). In the south window are scenes of Jesus being taken down from the cross (Mk 15.46, Lk. 23.53, Jn 19.38), the burial of Jesus (Mt. 27.60, Mk 15.46, Lk. 23.53, John 19.41–42), and the sealing of the tomb (Mt. 27.66).
 6 From south to north, they are dedicated respectively to St Peter, St Paul and St James. Each window is divided into five panels, each illustrating a verse from

the King James Version of the Bible. The southernmost window depicts faith, obedience and concern for others (from top to bottom: Acts 12.11, Jn 21.15–17, Mk 9.7, Mt. 14.31, Mt. 4.19). The two northern windows portray suffering, martyrdom and the need for faithfulness amidst affliction. The central window, from top to bottom, illustrates texts from 2 Cor. 4 vv. 11, 9, 5, 9, 8. The northernmost window, from top to bottom, illustrates texts from 2 Tim. 2.12, Mt. 20.22, Mt. 26.41, Mk 5.41, and another text (now missing).

7   Rev. 4.4.
8   Mt. 24.27.
9   For example, Lk. 1.78.
10   Jn 1.1–9.
11   Kavanaugh and Rodriguez, 1980, p. 294.
12   McLean, 2003, pp. 89–94.
13   Kavanaugh and Rodriguez, 1980, p. 303.
14   The southernmost of the nine tall windows in the east wall is of a discernibly different palette than the other east windows. The window in the south wall is clear glass, whereas the north window is stained glass.
15   From 'They came as dawn was breaking' by Rosalind Brown. Copyright © 1995, Rosalind Brown. Used by permission.
16   And there are more, if we study carefully the epitaphs dotted around the walls.
17   Lk. 2.35.
18   19.26–27.
19   We know nothing about her life between her baptism at age 13 years and her call by Aidan at age 33 years. It is entirely possible that she was married and widowed during this time.
20   Sherley-Price and Latham, 1988, p. 248.
21   Wolters, 1966, p. 166.
22   Translator anonymous, c.1915.
23   Ibid.
24   Ps. 84.5, New Jerusalem Bible.
25   Prayer attributed to St Columba.

Chapter 7: Contemplative Prayer: The Feretory
1   Sherley-Price and Latham, 1988, p. 263.
2   Webb and Farmer, 1998, p. 93.
3   Ibid.
4   Ibid., p. 98.
5   Ibid., p. 67.
6   Fowler, 1903, p. 4 (with rendition into contemporary English by the author).
7   Ibid. (with rendition into contemporary English by the author).
8   The Neville screen was built in the period 1372–80. Prior to the Reformation there were 107 statues of saints in the various niches on its east and west faces.
9   Mk 5.24–34.
10   Whilst this decision may seem strange today, it probably made perfect sense in medieval Christendom. Oswald had been patron of the Northumbrian Christian mission, a mission that Cuthbert pioneered in his day as a successor of Aidan. Oswald was also a martyr, which Cuthbert, for all his holiness, was not. The interment of a martyr's remains along with Cuthbert's therefore would have seemed fitting and would have further enhanced the perceived esteem in which

the shrine was eventually held. In fact, the tomb in the feretory is thought to contain the bones of various saints of Holy Island all of which were taken along with Cuthbert's remains by the monks who, in 875, fled from the Viking raids that made their island home unsafe.

11 See Ezekiel 1 and Revelation 4.

12 From *Banner Paintings of St Cuthbert and St Oswald for Durham Cathedral*, by Thetis Blacker, available for inspection at the visitors' desk in Durham Cathedral.

13 Church of England, 2005, p. 487.

14 See: Ezek. 1.5–11, Rev. 4.6–7; Mark is represented by the creature with the face of a lion, Matthew by the creature with a human face, John by the creature with the face of an eagle, and Luke by the creature with the face of an ox.

15 Isa. 6.2.

16 cf Ezek. 1.13, Rev. 4.5, Dan. 7.9–10.

17 On the west side: 'The angel said unto her fear not Mary for thou hast found favour with God' (Lk. 1.30). On the north side: 'Peter Andrew James John Philip Bartholomew Thomas Matthew James Thaddaeus Simon Matthias'. (This is the list of the names of the 12 disciples of Jesus, as given in Matthew's gospel [10.2–4], but with Matthias substituted for Judas. This is somewhat odd, as the substitution of Matthias for Judas after the death of the latter is given in the Lukan account in Acts 1.26. However, the Lukan list of disciples is somewhat different from the Mathean one, giving the names in a slightly different order and with the name of Judas son of James in the place of the name of Thaddeus. See Lk. 6.14–16, Acts 1.13). On the east side: 'Saint Michael the Archangel Saint Gabriel the Archangel'. On the south side: 'Angels & Archangels & Principalities & Powers & Dominions & Virtues & Thrones & Cherubim & Seraphim'. (These reflect the nine orders of angels outlined in the work of pseudo-Dionysius, which was adopted and made popular by medieval theologians. These orders were arranged into three hierarchies, each containing three 'choirs': Seraphim, Cherubim and Thrones; Dominations, Virtues and Powers; Principalities, Archangels and Angels. Only the third hierarchy [Principalities, Archangels and Angels] was understood to have direct involvement with the affairs of human beings. See Ferguson, 1972, p. 97, Cross and Livingstone, 1997, p. 62.)

18 Rev. 4.6–8.

19 Wolters, 1978.

20 See Chapter 5.

21 Wolters, 1978, pp .67–68.

22 Collect for St Cuthbert's Day, 20 March.

23 To be strictly historically accurate, the evidence that Cuthbert was a shepherd appears to be virtually non-existent. He probably came from a wealthy family that owned sheep, which is not quite the same as being a shepherd.

24 Ibid.

Chapter 8: Holy Places: Finding Ourselves and Finding God

1 Hawthorne, 1941, pp. 543–544. Hawthorne visited after the Cosin screen and Father Smith's organ had been removed, and before the present Scott screen was installed. In contrast to others at the time, he appears to have appreciated the openness that this afforded, seeing it as an advantage over all other cathedrals that he had visited. However, despite this, he did not appreciate the interior

architecture as a whole, describing it as a 'heavy grandeur' and concluding that 'it weighs upon the soul, instead of helping it to aspire' (p. 541).

2 Bryson, 1995. The opening of Chapter 24 relates his first visit to Durham. He was subsequently to become (and at the time of writing still is) Chancellor of Durham University.

3 The Cathedral gained over 51% of the vote – 15,819 votes were cast. See http://news.bbc.co.uk/1/hi/uk/1511841.stm

Bibliography

Adam, D. (2000) *The Cry of the Deer: Meditations on the Hymn of St Patrick*, London, Triangle.

Baedeker, K. (1910) *Baedeker's Great Britain*, 7th edn, Leipzig, Karl Baedeker.

Browne, G. (2002) *The Abbreviated Psalter of the Venerable Bede*, Grand Rapids, Eerdmans.

Bryson, B. (1995) *Notes from a Small Island*, London, Doubleday.

Church of England (2000) *Common Worship: Services and Prayers for the Church of England*, London, Church House Publishing.

Church of England (2005) *Common Worship: Daily Prayer*, London, Church House Publishing.

Cross, F. L. & Livingstone, E. A. (1997) *The Oxford Dictionary of the Christian Church*, Oxford, Oxford.

Davies, O., O'Loughlin, T. & Mackey, J. (1999) *Celtic Christianity*, New York, Paulist Press.

De Waal, E. (1984) *Seeking God: The Way of St Benedict*, London, Collins.

Duncan, B. (2000) *Pray Your Way*, London, Darton, Longman & Todd.

Ferguson, G. (1972) *Signs & Symbols in Christian Art*, Oxford, Oxford.

Fowler, J. T. (1903) *Rites of Durham: Being a Description or Brief Declaration of All the Ancient Monuments, Rites & Customs Belonging or Being within the Monastical Church of Durham before the Suppression. Written 1593*, Durham, Andrews.

Fry, T., Baker, I., Horner, T., Raabe, A. & Sheridan, M. (1982) *The Rule of St Benedict in English*, Collegeville, The Liturgical Press.

Hawthorne, N. (1941) *The English Notebooks*, New York, Modern Language Association of America.

Kavanaugh, K. & Rodriguez, O. (1980) *The Collected Works of St Teresa of Avila*, Washington, Institute of Carmelite Studies.

Marner, D. (2000) *St Cuthbert: His Life and Cult in Medieval Durham*, London, The British Library.

McGreal, W. (1999) *At the Fountain of Elijah: The Carmelite Tradition*, London, DLT.

McLean, J. (2003) *Towards Mystical Union: A Modern Commentary on the Mystical Text 'The Interior Castle' by St Teresa of Avila*, London, St Paul's.

Miller, C. (1995) *Praying the Eucharist*, London, SPCK.

Munitiz, J. A. & Endean, P. (1996) *Saint Ignatius of Loyola: Personal Writings*, Harmondsworth, Penguin.

Otto, R. (1980) *The Idea of the Holy*, Oxford, Oxford.

Pritchard, J. (2002) *How to Pray: A Practical Handbook*, London, SPCK.

Rice, F. (1994) *The Hermit of Finchale*, Pentland Press, Edinburgh.

Sadgrove, M. (2006) *A Pilgrim in Durham Cathedral*, Norwich, Jarrold.

Sadgrove, M. (2007) The Durham Book. In Gameson, R. (Ed.) *Treasures of Durham University Library*, London, Third Millenium.

Sherley-Price, L. & Latham, R. E. (1988) *Bede: A History of the English Church and People*, London, Penguin.

Silf, M. (2004) *Companions of Christ: Ignatian Spirituality for Everyday Living*, Norwich, Canterbury Press.

Slee, N. (2004) *Praying Like a Woman*, London, SPCK.

Society of Saint Francis (1996) *Celebrating Common Prayer: Pocket Version*, London, Mowbray.

Stancliffe, D. (2003) *The Pilgrim Prayerbook*, London, Continuum.

Stanwood, P. G. (1967) *John Cosin: A Collection of Private Devotions*, Oxford, Oxford University Press.

Tobin, J. (1991) *George Herbert: The Complete English Poems*, London, Penguin.

Ward, B. (1973) *The Prayers and Meditations of Saint Anselm, with the Proslogion*, Harmondsworth, Penguin.

Ward, B. (2003) *The Desert Fathers: Sayings of the Early Christian Monks*, London, Penguin.

Warner, M. (2004) *The Habit of Holiness: Daily Prayer*, London, Continuum.

Webb, J. F. & Farmer, D. H. (1998) *The Age of Bede*, London, Penguin.

Wolters, C. (1966) *Julian of Norwich: Revelations of Divine Love*, London, Penguin.

Wolters, C. (1978) *The Cloud of Unknowing and Other Works*, London, Penguin.

Index

Aidan 48, 55, 56, 62, 85, 101, 103, 104,
114, 118, 129
annunciation 43, 84, 86–7, 97, 135,
147

baptism 24, 45, 47–9
of Jesus 20, 46, 52
Bede 8–9, 55, 81–3, 90–3, 97–8, 110,
114, 125, 136–7
Benedict Biscop 48, 55, 85

Coifi 48, 55
Columba 118
communion of saints 33, 59, 128, 136,
138, 144
contemplation 9, 12, 31, 85, 136–42
Cosin, John 61, 63
cross
cathedral in the shape of 10–11
death of Jesus on 45
empty 84, 86, 88, 92, 110, 114
foot of 87–9, 94, 113
Heavenfield 133–4
instrument and place of execution
4, 94, 97, 99, 110, 114
procession/journey of Jesus to 88,
116
sign of the 31, 56, 98, 121
suffering of Jesus on 67, 87, 93,
111
taking up 45, 89, 91, 116, 136, 138
words of Jesus from 21, 67
Cuthbert 8–10, 55, 79–83, 102–6,
122–42, 146–8, 151

dark side 1–2, 4, 60, 80

Eucharist 23–5, 45–50, 84, 92, 131,
133

Godric of Finchale 13

healing 8, 20, 81, 90, 133
Hild 85, 114–15, 117, 147
see also icon(s), of Hild

icon(s) 23, 24, 31, 37
Durham Cathedral as an 5
of Hild 101, 104, 107, 114–15, 117
iconography of Cuthbert's coffin 135,
153
incarnation 3, 19, 45–6, 58, 68, 77,
86–90, 92–3, 96, 142

Jesus prayer 13, 31, 97
John the Baptist 68, 98, 103
John the beloved disciple 27, 51, 87–8,
103, 107, 113–14
journey
following Christ 45, 46
of Christ 78, 116
towards God/Christ 108, 150
inner 14, 108, 121, 150
life 5, 108, 120
pilgrimage 107–8, 116–18, 120–1,
127
see also pilgrimage
Julian of Norwich 41, 116

lectio divina 9, 16–17

Margaret of Scotland viii, 103–4, 107,
113–15, 117, 147

163